THE GREAT CHIEFS

THE GREAT CHIEFS

By the Editors of

TIME-LIFE BOOKS

with text by

Benjamin Capps

TIME-LIFE BOOKS / ALEXANDRIA, VIRGINIA

Time-Life Books Inc.
is a wholly owned subsidiary of

TIME INCORPORATED

Founder: Henry R. Luce 1898-1967

Editor-in-Chief: Henry Anatole Grunwald
President: J. Richard Munro
Chairman of the Board: Ralph P. Davidson
Corporate Editor: Jason McManus
Group Vice President, Books: Reginald K. Brack Jr.
Vice President, Books: George Artandi

TIME-LIFE BOOKS INC.

Editor: George Constable
Executive Editor: George Daniels
Editorial General Manager: Neal Goff
Director of Design: Louis Klein
Editorial Board: Dale M. Brown, Roberta Conlan,
Ellen Phillips, Gerry Schremp, Gerald Simons,
Rosalind Stubenberg, Kit van Tulleken, Henry Woodhead
Director of Research: Phyllis K. Wise
Director of Photography: John Conrad Weiser

President: William J. Henry
Senior Vice President: Christopher T. Linen
Vice Presidents: Stephen L. Bair, Robert A. Ellis,
John M. Fahey Jr., Juanita T. James, James L. Mercer,
Joanne A. Pello, Paul R. Stewart, Christian Strasser

THE OLD WEST

Editor: George Constable
EDITORIAL STAFF FOR "THE GREAT CHIEFS"
Assistant Editor: Joan Mebane
Picture Editor: Mary Y. Steinbauer
Text Editor: Valerie Moolman
Designer: Herbert H. Quarmby
Staff Writers: Lee Greene, Sam Halper, Kirk Landers,
Robert Tschirky, Eve Wengler
Chief Researcher: June O. Goldberg
Researchers: Loretta Britten, Jane Coughran, Mary Leverty,
Donna Lucey, Michael Luftman, Archer Mayor, Nancy Miller,
Mary Kay Moran, Vivian Stephens
Design Assistant: Faye Eng
Copy Coordinators: Barbara H. Fuller, Gregory Weed
Picture Coordinator: Susan Spiller
Editorial Assistant: Lisa Berger

EDITORIAL OPERATIONS
Design: Ellen Robling (assistant director)
Copy Room: Diane Ullius
Editorial Operations: Caroline A. Boubin (manager)
Production: Celia Beattie
Quality Control: James J. Cox (director), Sally Collins
Library: Louise D. Forstall

THE AUTHOR: Benjamin Capps, a freelancer who makes his home in Grand Prairie, Texas, has written nine books dealing with the Great Plains in the 19th Century, including *The Indians* for TIME-LIFE BOOKS. Shortly before undertaking *The Great Chiefs* he completed *The Warren Wagontrain Raid,* a study of an 1871 episode that marked a high point of Kiowa resistance against encroaching Texans.

THE COVER: This portrait of Crow chief He Who Jumps over Every One, astride a war pony whose feather plumage matches his own, was created by artist George Catlin in the 1830s. At the time, the leaders of the Western tribes were barely aware of the stirrings of a white horde on the margins of their dominion. By the end of the 19th Century, the threat had swept them to ruin and only elegies remained — none more masterful than E. S. Curtis' frontispiece photograph of Chief Red Hawk. The Sioux leader had helped vanquish Custer at the Little Bighorn in 1876 and lived to see his tribe suffer a countermassacre at Wounded Knee in 1890.

CORRESPONDENTS: Elisabeth Kraemer-Singh (Bonn); Margot Hapgood, Dorothy Bacon (London); Miriam Hsia, Susan Jonas, Lucy T. Voulgaris (New York); Maria Vincenza Aloisi, Josephine du Brusle (Paris); Ann Natanson (Rome). Valuable assistance was also provided by: Judy Aspinall, Lesley Coleman, Karin B. Pearce (London); Carolyn T. Chubet, Christina Lieberman (New York); Mimi Murphy (Rome).

Other Publications:

YOUR HOME
THE ENCHANTED WORLD
THE KODAK LIBRARY OF
  CREATIVE PHOTOGRAPHY
GREAT MEALS IN MINUTES
THE CIVIL WAR
PLANET EARTH
COLLECTOR'S LIBRARY OF THE
  CIVIL WAR
THE EPIC OF FLIGHT
THE GOOD COOK
THE SEAFARERS
WORLD WAR II
HOME REPAIR AND IMPROVEMENT

For information on and a full description
of any of the Time-Life Books series
listed at right, please write:
Reader Information
Time-Life Books
541 North Fairbanks Court
Chicago, Illinois 60611

*This volume is one of a series that
chronicles the history of the American West
from the early 16th Century to the end of
the 19th Century.*

Library of Congress Cataloging in Publication Data
Time-Life Books
  The great chiefs / by the editors of Time-Life Books; with text
by Benjamin Capps. — New York: Time-Life Books, c1975.
  240 p.:ill. (some col.); 28 cm. — (The Old West)
  Bibliography: p. 236-237.
  Includes index.
  1. Indians of North America — The West — Biography.
  2. Indians of North America — The West — Wars.
  3. The West — Biography.   I. Capps, Benjamin, 1922-
  II. Title. III. Series: The Old West (Alexandria, Va.)
E78.W5T55 1975   970'.004'97   75-744
ISBN 0-8094-1494-5
ISBN 0-8094-1493-7 (lib. bdg.)
ISBN 0-8094-1492-9 (retail ed.)

CONTENTS

1 | An assembly of eagles
6

2 | Guerrilla fighters in a rugged domain
54

3 | Final champion of Comanche glory
101

4 | Protecting a way of life
130

5 | Pacifist on the warpath
162

6 | The threatened world of Sitting Bull
192

Credits 234   Acknowledgments 236   Bibliography 236   Index 238

1 | An assembly of eagles

Proud, joyously combative, free as the wind—these were the chiefs of the Old West at the beginning of the 19th Century, when the buffalo ran 30 million strong and the white frontier had barely vaulted the Appalachians.

Popular imagination saw them as powerful feudal lords, reigning over multitudes of bloodthirsty but obedient subjects. In fact, there were neither monarchs nor multitudes between the Mississippi and the far side of the Rockies. The 200,000 Indians of that region were fragmented into bands and tribes ranging in size from a few dozen members to several thousand. Each group regulated its affairs by a system of leadership that was as supple as the Indians' nomadic life style itself.

The relationship of Western tribesmen to their chiefs was recognized as early as 1805 in the journals of the explorers Meriwether Lewis and William Clark: "Each individual is his own master, and the only control to which his conduct is subjected is the advice of a chief, supported by his influence over the rest of the tribe." The chief's power was anything but absolute: "His commands have no effect on those who incline to disobey."

Only by earning the respect of his peers could a man become chief. Ambitious warriors strove to emulate the eagle, the high-flying predator whose feathers were prized symbols of bold exploits. The warrior who amassed feathers enough to sport a trailing war bonnet was well on his way to attaining a chieftainship.

Despite their limited authority, the chiefs were able to provide remarkably resourceful leadership when called upon to face the inexorable tide of white invasion. Some resisted with uncompromising ferocity, like Geronimo of the Apaches, who battled settlers and soldiers for more than 30 years. Others, like Washakie of the Shoshonis, invested all their hopes in cooperation, earning less fame than those who resisted to the bitter end yet leaving a deep imprint on history. Still others were fervent idealists: Chief Joseph of the Nez Percés attempted desperately to avoid war with the white man, but when a long list of injustices culminated in a ruthless attack by the United States Army, he fought until his band was nearly destroyed. Even then he cried out for peace and understanding: "I hope that no more groans of wounded men and women will ever go to the ear of the Great Spirit above, and that all people may be one people."

No artist ever captured the essence of Indian leaders more sensitively than George Catlin, a Pennsylvania-born portraitist who set out in 1830 to preserve a memory of the customs and character of "the noble races of red men, melting away at the approach of civilization." During the course of a six-year Western odyssey, Catlin visited 146 tribes and painted the portraits of scores of chiefs, including those depicted here. In their raiment of feathers and buffalo robes they appeared indomitable, but already they were beset with tribulations that no chief could long withstand. "To use their own very beautiful expression," Catlin observed, "they are fast traveling to the shades of their fathers, towards the setting sun."

BLACK ROCK, BAND CHIEF OF THE TETON SIOUX
The majestic leader of the Neecoweegee band, which roamed the upper reaches of the
Missouri, was painted by Catlin with "the battles of his life emblazoned on his robe."

SMOKE, HEAD CHIEF OF THE PONCAS
"A noble specimen of native dignity and philosophy" was Catlin's description of the
Ponca leader, whose people lived near the union of the Missouri and Niobrara rivers.

CLERMONT, HEAD CHIEF OF THE OSAGES
Seated on a rock throne, the chief of the Osages — a small tribe on the southern plains
— cradles a war club rendered more lethal by a metal blade obtained from white traders.

WOLF CHIEF, HEAD CHIEF OF THE MANDANS
"A haughty, austere, and overbearing man," said Catlin of this tribal leader, whose
people lived along the upper Missouri in lodges constructed of earth-covered logs.

MOLE IN THE FOREHEAD, BAND CHIEF OF THE PAWNEES
Named, as many Indians were, for a physical trait, this "very distinguished warrior"
headed a Pawnee contingent whose lands lay between the Platte and Kansas rivers.

CHARGER, HEAD CHIEF OF THE YANKTON SIOUX
An exemplar of valor in a northern plains tribe that Catlin called "one of the most
numerous and powerful" he had seen, Charger suffered nine gunshot wounds in battle.

EAGLE'S RIBS, WAR CHIEF OF THE PIEGAN BLACKFEET
War leader of a band living by the mouth of the Yellowstone River, Eagle's Ribs boasted to a startled Catlin of "eight scalps taken from the heads of trappers and traders."

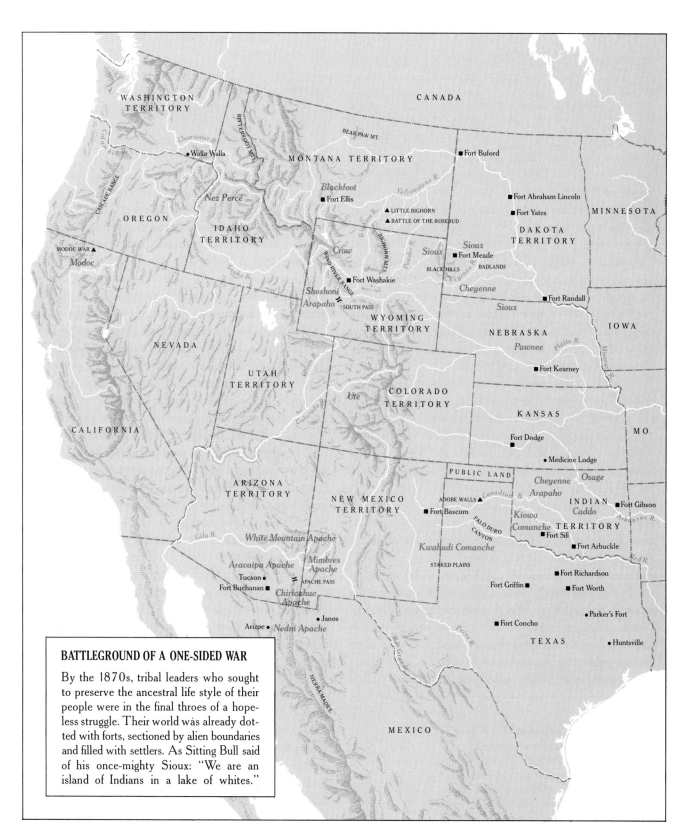

CANADA

WASHINGTON
TERRITORY

BEAR PAW MT.

MONTANA TERRITORY

■ Fort Buford

Clearwater R.

• Walla Walla

Blackfoot

Nez Percé
■ Fort Ellis

▲ LITTLE BIGHORN
▲ BATTLE OF THE ROSEBUD

■ Fort Abraham Lincoln

■ Fort Yates

MINNESOTA

OREGON

IDAHO
TERRITORY

Crow

Sioux   *Sioux*
■ Fort Meade

DAKOTA
TERRITORY

MODOC WAR ▲

Modoc

Shoshoni
Arapaho
SOUTH PASS

■ Fort Washakie

BLACK HILLS   BADLANDS

Cheyenne

Sioux

■ Fort Randall

IOWA

NEVADA

UTAH
TERRITORY

WYOMING
TERRITORY

Ute

COLORADO
TERRITORY

NEBRASKA

Pawnee

■ Fort Kearney

CALIFORNIA

KANSAS

MO

Fort Dodge
■

ARIZONA
TERRITORY

NEW MEXICO
TERRITORY

ADOBE WALLS ▲

■ Fort Bascom

• Medicine Lodge

PUBLIC LAND

Cheyenne
Arapaho

Osage

INDIAN
Caddo

■ Fort Gibson

TERRITORY

Kiowa
Comanche

■ Fort Sill

White Mountain Apache

Kwahadi Comanche

■ Fort Arbuckle

Aravaipa Apache
Tucson •
Fort Buchanan ■

Mimbres
Apache
APACHE PASS

STAKED PLAINS

■ Fort Richardson

Fort Griffin ■   ■ Fort Worth

Chiricahua
Apache

• Janos

Arizpe •   *Nedni Apache*

• Parker's Fort

■ Fort Concho

SIERRA MADRE

TEXAS   • Huntsville

MEXICO

BATTLEGROUND OF A ONE-SIDED WAR

By the 1870s, tribal leaders who sought
to preserve the ancestral life style of their
people were in the final throes of a hopeless struggle. Their world was already dot-
ted with forts, sectioned by alien boundaries
and filled with settlers. As Sitting Bull said
of his once-mighty Sioux: "We are an
island of Indians in a lake of whites."

arrow sunk deep into its flesh — not an arrow of their own, but one whose shaft bore the markings of the Osages, another long-time enemy. Their presence so near the Kiowa camp was ominous. The hunters galloped back to warn their principal chief. All revelry ceased at once. Islandman posted sentries and supervised the building of adobe breastworks for defense.

Days passed and no attack came. Finally the Kiowas began to breathe more easily. What they had feared to be hostiles in force was, they concluded, a handful of Osage hunters prowling the plains for meat.

By now the grass near the camp had been nibbled low by the herd of Kiowa mounts, and there was need to move. Islandman took council with the few leaders who had not gone off with the raiding party and agreed to permit the tribe to split into several groups. The buffalo hunters again set off on their own. Another group headed for a known range of wild horses; there they would hobble their brood mares in the path of stallions too wild to be captured, and thus breed up the hardiness of the Kiowas' domestic herds. Islandman himself led another contingent — comprised mainly of old men and women, young mothers and children — through a mountain gap to a green valley on Otter Creek.

Late in the afternoon of the day that Islandman pitched his new camp, some girls went to the creek for water. As they cupped their hands to drink from a still pool, a pebble dropped from the rocks above. They looked up: no one was there. But when the ripples smoothed away, a girl bending toward the water saw, to her horror, not only her own reflection but also the wavering image of a strange warrior.

Trying to act as though nothing was amiss, the girls went quietly back to camp to spread the alarm. On hearing their report, Islandman and the other old men smiled and dismissed the incident as a prank played by some of the boys to exploit the girls' fears after the scare caused by the Osage arrow.

Early the next morning a youth left the camp to lead his family's ponies to pasture. Something moved behind a rock; as his eyes followed the movement into the gloom, he was appalled to see the shaved head of an Osage. He ran back, screaming, to wake the others. Stumbling half-dressed from their tipis, Islandman's people found their camp already aswarm with Osages. "To the rocks! To the rocks!" yelled Islandman as he

himself ran in that direction. His panic-stricken people tried to follow. Some ran headlong into the enemy, who slashed and stabbed with long knives, mercilessly ripping the throats of young and old. There were individual acts of heroism, but very few. As the keeper of the *taime* scuttled for safety, leaving the sacred idol tied to a tipi pole, his wife tried to rescue it and was butchered. Sensing its value, the Osages tore the *taime* from her dying hands.

Without their warriors and without effective leadership, the Kiowas were routed in a shameful defeat. While many women and children were slaughtered, only five of the men lost their lives. Islandman escaped with a minor wound. Not a single one of the attackers died — and this in the camp of the Kiowas' principal chief.

When the killing was done, the Osages cut off the heads of the dead and placed them in the Kiowas' own brass cooking buckets. They then carefully arranged the buckets in rows amidst the devastation of the camp and left them there as a greeting for the returning Kiowa warriors. After that, they fired the tipis and left, taking with them the *taime* and two captive children.

The Kiowa fighting men came back from the land of the Utes expecting a joyous reception, for they had fared well. Instead, they found a scene of unbridled grief. The surviving women were mourning the dead by slashing their faces and bodies until the blood flowed as it had on the day of the massacre. And on the grim face of every man could be read the same thought: that Islandman was not worthy of being their principal chief. It was an issue that had to be aired in council.

Summoned by a camp crier, every man who had any claim to importance in the tribe — as orator, warrior, hunter or healer — came together around a fire, smoked a ceremonial pipe in silence and prepared to discuss the dereliction of the chief and the consequent necessity of choosing a successor. One of the older men, respected by all for his wisdom, arose and spoke first.

Islandman, he said, had failed utterly in his responsibility to the tribe. Not only had he exercised poor judgment in permitting the reduced camp at Rainy Mountain Creek to break up into several smaller groups, not only had he neglected to take the minimal precaution of posting sentries when Osages were about, but he had even failed to make a stand and inspire others by his personal example. It had been his duty to place the welfare of his tribe above all else, including his own life, yet he had fled in terror before the enemy. This having been bluntly said, and unanimously agreed to, the council members spoke of Islandman no more, nor would they ever heed his voice again. There would be no formal punishment for him: he would simply slip into obscurity and become an ordinary tribesman, a man who had for all time forfeited his influence and following. Far more important now than Islandman was the question of replacement.

Members of the council who wished to make statements rose to do so in an order befitting their years and experience. There was no rigidly prescribed sequence, but always the older men spoke first and then the men of middle years. Even a young warrior might, after his elders had spoken, ask and receive permission to express his views if he had some bold deeds and a measure of eloquence to his credit.

Each man was heard with the utmost courtesy for as long as he wished to speak, and each viewpoint was solemnly considered, for the art of persuasion was the essence of such meetings and a man was entitled to his chance to persuade. No orator was interrupted and no council member was permitted to leave the session until consensus declared it recessed. This was custom in most of the tribes that roamed the Western plains. In one such meeting a council member suffered a severe nosebleed and could do nothing but stop up his nostrils and choke down the blood, almost suffocating in the process, until the meeting was over.

The Kiowa council dwelt at length on the requirements for the office of principal chief and on the qualities desired in the man named to fulfill it. To begin with, he must have a record of outstanding accomplishment in war; although in his new role he would not himself be a tactical leader, he would be expected to set an example of courage if circumstance brought war to his people, as it had to Islandman. He must possess a compelling personality that would draw others to him and inspire their loyalty and respect. Indeed, respect was his sole source of power, and to be truly effective he must be a man of great wealth—the owner of many horses obtained by leading raids. Moreover, he must have demonstrated his generosity by giving feasts and providing food, horses and buffalo hides to those who

An Indian family treks through the Wichita Mountains in this painting of the Kiowa heartland by soldier-artist Hermann Stieffel. Driven from the northern plains by the Sioux in the early 19th Century, the Kiowas reasserted their power in a range extending from central Kansas into Texas.

Destined to lead the Kiowas for more than three decades, Little Mountain strikes a pose of stolid confidence for artist George Catlin in 1834, a year after rising to power in the wake of the massacre by the Osages.

the Indians' lands were still unfenced and unplowed, their life was not unchanged, and the pace of change would quicken with every passing year.

In the summer of 1834, a force of U.S. dragoons under Colonel Henry Dodge rode through the lands of the Kiowas, Comanches, Cherokees, Creeks, Osages and Wichitas to establish friendly relations with these tribes, whose hostilities had been interfering with white trade and travel on the plains. At a Wichita village Dodge met a visiting contingent of Kiowas, led by Little Mountain, and in the face of their initial suspicion he quickly explained that the government wished to establish a lasting peace with them. Little Mountain greeted the strangers with affable dignity. Although he had never before encountered American troops and considered them decidedly bizarre in appearance, he was prepared to deal with them as he would with a peaceful delegation from a neighboring tribe.

In a grand council, the colonel offered the Kiowas generous trading privileges in return for the safe passage of U.S. citizens traveling the Santa Fe Trail. To sweeten the proposition he bestowed an unexpected gift: a Kiowa girl who had been taken captive by the Osages during the massacre of the previous year. The soldiers had ransomed her for the purpose of bringing about a friendly meeting with Kiowa leaders.

Little Mountain was extremely gratified. "White men and brethren," he said, "this day is the most interesting period of our existence. The Great Spirit has caused a light to shine all around us so that we can see each other. The Great Spirit has sent us to see these white men and brothers. Kiowas, take them by the hand and use them well. They are your friends; they have brought home your lost relation."

In this atmosphere of brotherhood and trust it was not difficult for Dodge to persuade Little Mountain and 14 other Kiowa chiefs to accompany the dragoon force to Fort Gibson some 200 miles to the east. There the Kiowas received presents of food and clothing, and promised to cease their depredations along the Santa Fe Trail. There, too, they held peace talks with representatives of the Cherokee, Creek, Choctaw and Osage tribes, whose lands lay to the east — close enough to the frontier so that whites were desirous of avoiding intertribal disturbances. Little Mountain was able to make a most felicitous exchange with a chief of the Osages:

one fine Kiowa horse in return for the priceless *taime.*

For well over a decade the Kiowas kept their promise to the white men and let travelers pass unmolested along the great trail. But they did not hesitate to swoop down into Texas on raiding expeditions against the hated white men there who seemed intent upon thrusting their way up into Kiowa-Comanche territory.

Life continued much as before until gold was discovered in California in 1848. Thereafter, seemingly endless trains of covered wagons came rolling across the Kiowa range, bringing a devastating cholera epidemic and laying waste the grasslands alongside the Santa Fe Trail. Smaller strikes elsewhere in the West maintained the cavalcade of fortune hunters through the middle of the 1850s. Then, in 1858, gold was found in large quantities in the Pikes Peak region of Colorado.

With that, the trek across the plains developed into a stampede. Within one year some 100,000 white adventurers of every stripe swarmed unchecked across the Kiowas' hunting grounds, despoiling the Earth Mother with a recklessness that the Indians found appalling. They chopped down trees and wasted precious wood along the trails. Their horses, mules and oxen gnawed bare the good grazing land. Hunters shot buffalo and antelope from their wagons, and when there was nothing left in sight to shoot they ranged far afield in search of game. When they killed too much, as often they did, they left the unwanted carcasses to rot and moved on, killing more. Some travelers gave up their quest for gold and set up farms, ranches and even fledgling towns on the tribe's accustomed range.

The Kiowas, enraged by the intrusions and devastation, fell upon settlers and travelers alike — and also picked up the tempo and ferocity of their raids into Texas. Late in 1858, at a Kiowa encampment on the Arkansas River, a government-appointed Indian agent named Robert Miller delivered a warning to Little Mountain. Unless the Kiowas and their allies ceased their depredations, Miller threatened, the government would send troops to punish them.

For the first time, Little Mountain spoke hostile words to a white official. Admitting his warriors' raids only indirectly, he said scornfully: "The white chief is a fool. He is a coward. When my young men, to keep their women and children from starving, take a cup of sugar or coffee from the white men passing through our

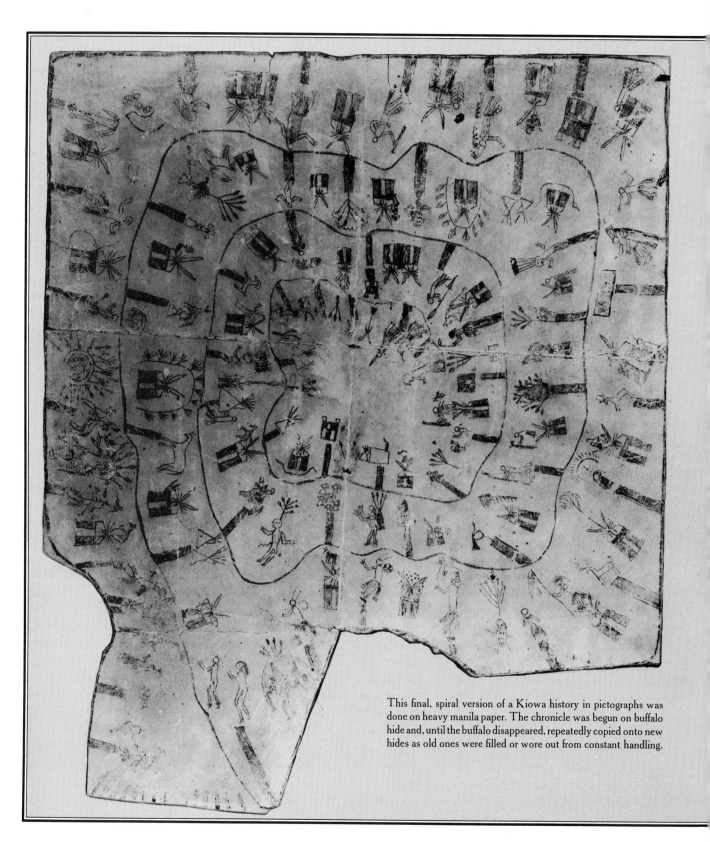

This final, spiral version of a Kiowa history in pictographs was done on heavy manila paper. The chronicle was begun on buffalo hide and, until the buffalo disappeared, repeatedly copied onto new hides as old ones were filled or wore out from constant handling.

A sixty-year picture history of a valiant people

Through good times and bad, the Kiowas were keenly interested in keeping track of their history to reinforce a sense of tribal identity. Since they lacked a written language, they recorded important events in cumulative chronicles like the one opposite, which expresses almost 60 years of Kiowa history in an ingenious visual shorthand. It was started in 1833 by Little Mountain, soon to be principal chief. After his death in 1866, the record was continued by his nephew, who made a final copy in spiral form, beginning at the lower left and ending in the center.

Each year in the long saga is represented by two images—one recalling an event of the winter, the other showing a summer incident. Wintertime entries were drawn above a black bar symbolizing a dead blade of grass. Summer occurrences were usually depicted above an image of the sacred lodge *(below, far right)* in which the annual sun dance was held.

A few of the entries, such as the one second from right below, reflect the personal concerns of the chronicler, but mostly they document vicissitudes of great moment to the whole tribe—a victory over an enemy, for instance, or the death of a chief. During the long nights in winter camp, the chronicler would call to other men, "Come and smoke"; a pipe would be passed, and each warrior present would elaborate on the circumstances surrounding a particular pictograph, thus bringing the past to life again.

In the chronicle the destructive effect of an alien culture is registered only indirectly — by the disappearance of the sun dance symbol near the end. Its absence reflects the banning of the ceremony by reservation authorities — a bitter blow to the tribesmen.

In 1892, Little Mountain's nephew turned the chronicle over to the United States Army, so the power that had subjugated his tribe might at least preserve the memory of what the Kiowas had been in times gone by.

ENTRIES FROM THE KIOWA CHRONICLE

A butcher knife circled by severed heads represents the 1833 massacre of Kiowa women and children by the Osages. The disaster—at a site in the Wichita Mountains later known to the tribe as Cutthroat Gap—was the second entry on the chronicle.

The Kiowa girl memorialized by this pictograph returned to her people in 1834, a year after she was taken captive by the Osages. The joyous reunion was brought about by Colonel Henry Dodge, who ransomed the girl to facilitate peace parleys with the tribe.

Placed over a dead blade of grass indicating a winter entry, a knife-wielding warrior symbolizes an incident of 1843, when a man stabbed his wife for riding behind Little Mountain in a procession. The woman, who had acted at the chief's invitation, survived.

An auspicious manifestation of the spirits in 1858 is marked by a sun dance lodge with a forked stick protruding from it. The stick was left in the ground following the previous year's sun dance, and when the Kiowas returned, they found that it had taken root.

country, killing and driving away our buffalo, the white chief is angry and threatens to send his soldiers. I have looked for them a long time, but they have not come. His heart is a woman's. I have spoken."

So the Kiowas continued their attacks. No reprisal came, for much of the white army was occupied with the Civil War. By the summer of 1864, drivers of freight wagons were afraid to cross the plains, and the Denver area began running short of food. Mail service to Santa Fe was stopped because of Kiowa strikes against stage stations and coaches.

In July, Kiowa war chief White Bear and a party of warriors attacked a ranch a few miles from Fort Lyon, Colorado, then moved on to a nearby stage station where they killed four men. A few days later White Bear led a raid into a settlement near Menard, Texas, and killed several residents. That same month, another war party of Kiowas attacked a wagon train in Kansas and killed 10 teamsters. In October, growing ever more audacious, Kiowa raiders joined a force of Comanches and ravaged a series of settlements on Elm Creek near Fort Belknap, Texas, this time killing 11 people and capturing seven others.

If the raiders thought themselves secure from retaliation, they were mistaken. It came from Colonel Kit Carson—the famed trapper and scout—who was serving in the Southwest with the New Mexico Volunteers, organized to protect frontiersmen against Indian depredations. In the fall of 1864 Carson was ordered by his commanding officer, General James H. Carleton, to launch a slashing punitive attack on the marauders.

By November most of the Indians were in their winter camps, no longer raiding because their horses, subsisting on paltry winter grass and cottonwood bark, were too weak for spirited action. Early that month Carson rode east from Cimarron, New Mexico, with a regiment made up of 14 officers, 321 cavalrymen and 72 Indian scouts—Utes and Jicarilla Apaches who had no love for Kiowas but understood their thinking and tactics. Entirely unaware of their approach, Little Mountain was encamped, along with some Comanches, on the Canadian River in the Texas Panhandle.

When Carson's force struck early one cold morning, Little Mountain—unlike Islandman in his moment of crisis—swiftly organized his warriors into an orderly retreat, protecting the women and children, and sent a

courier galloping downriver to call for help from neighboring Kiowa and Comanche camps. He himself had his horse shot out from under him while leading the defense, but he continued to rally his warriors as reinforcements arrived from one camp after another.

The battle raged all day over the river bottoms and surrounding hills. At intervals the white soldiers blew bugle calls as signals to each other; a Kiowa warrior who had become the owner of a bugle captured in previous hostilities responded by blowing contradictory calls until the soldiers were totally confused.

Carson's troops might well have been overrun had they not brought along two 12-pound howitzers that fired explosive shells and were horribly effective in breaking up concentrations of warriors. The Kiowas scattered, circled the whites' position, and re-entered the village they had fled. There they succeeded in saving their precious horse herd; but the soldiers again put them to flight with the deadly howitzers. After the withdrawal of the Indian forces, Carson set fire to the 176 lodges of their camp, burned all their dried meat and other winter provisions, and all their buffalo robes and clothes. This done, the soldiers retired in good order. Three of Carson's men were killed in the engagement and 15 wounded. The Kiowa-Comanche forces, by Carson's count, lost 60 killed and 150 wounded.

It was a stunning blow to Little Mountain. He knew that the white attack would have been repelled if it had not been for the devastating howitzers. But against these terrible weapons there was no defense. What was a man to do in the face of such unthinkable force?

In 1865, Little Mountain recommended to his council that there be another peace meeting with the United States. At Bluff Creek near the mouth of the Little Arkansas River, the Kiowas and their Comanche allies met in October with a U.S. delegation headed by Colonel Jesse Leavenworth. Little Mountain and other tribal leaders listened with grave skepticism as government spokesmen tried to explain that it would be in the best interests of all parties for the Kiowas to confine themselves to certain areas distant from the main travel routes: specifically, lands south of the Canadian River and north of the Red.

Little Mountain protested. How could the whites parcel out lands that did not belong to them? Nevertheless, in the interests of peace with such a powerful people, he and six other Kiowa leaders signed the treaty on the government's terms, giving up all claims to western Texas, southwestern Kansas, eastern New Mexico and southeastern Colorado. The pact left them with the southwestern part of Oklahoma—then called Indian Territory—and most of the Texas Panhandle, which fortunately included the best of their traditional buffalo-hunting grounds. In return for their acceptance of limits on their roving and their promise of future docility, they were to be given annual presents of hunting rifles, staple foods, utensils and tools, seeds for planting, blankets and—of all things—suits.

They left the meeting not realizing the nature of the bargain they had made. After all, they still had their best buffalo range, and the presents of foodstuffs and other items would help to see them through hard times. The hints of the peace commissioners that they settle down, farm and become educated in white men's ways registered only dimly. In their innocence, with only the vaguest understanding of the terms of the treaty, they had committed themselves to life on a reservation.

The placing of troublesome—or inconveniently located—Indians on reservations was a long-standing U.S. policy. Between 1790 and 1834, Congress had passed a series of laws called the Indian Trade and Intercourse Acts, aimed at guaranteeing the Indians a safe homeland and gradually narrowing the gulf between the two cultures. Under the legislation, reservation-bound Indians were to be subject to their own laws rather than those of the United States, and an agent—appointed by the President—would serve as liaison with the tribe. His duties included dispensing provisions—called annuities—arresting traffickers in liquor, evicting trespassers attempting to settle on the reservations and arranging consultations between Indian tribes or between Indian chiefs and government representatives. Working under the agent's supervision—when the system functioned according to plan—were teachers, carpenters, blacksmiths and farmers, whose task was to abet the Indians in the various arts of civilization.

This was all very well in theory, but the handouts of food and other goods tended to drain the initiative of the Indians. Nor could the people of the Plains tribes reasonably be expected to take up farming. Such drudgery was anathema to horseborne knights who gloried in combat; and in any case, the lands allotted to them were often too arid for cultivation by the techniques they were taught. And as for the supposedly iron-clad guarantee of reservation lands, it was a fiction. Time and time again, the government found ways to induce the Indians to give up territory that had been described to them as a permanent homeland.

This was the system to which Little Mountain and his fellow chiefs had unwittingly committed the Kiowas. Perhaps it was fortunate for their principal chief that he died a natural death the following year. For more than three decades he had served his people honorably and bravely. He had kept his tribe unified, even if the world into which he had been born was no longer intact. White Bear said of Little Mountain: "He did all he could to make peace, and kept talking and talking, but the white man kept doing something bad to him, and he was in so much misery that he died."

For months after Little Mountain's death uncertainty about a successor persisted in Kiowa council meetings. The tribe had many strong personalities who made their voices heard, but they could not agree even after many council sessions. Two factions emerged, and their differences ran deep: Was it to be peace, or was it to be war? Should they become copies of white men, with schools and houses and the planting and plowing of fields? Or should they ignore the treaty that had been signed and pursue the life of their forefathers, raiding wherever and whenever they pleased?

Tacit in all their discussions was a recognition that white influence would loom large in the future. The only real question was how to cope with it—or, more specifically, what sort of leader was best suited to cope with it. If the future course was to resist the whites and all that they stood for, perhaps the great war chief Sitting Bear could best unite them. He was the leader of the Society of the Ten Bravest, the Kiowas' most elite military organization, and his courage was legendary. But, though deeply respected, Sitting Bear was in his sixties—and it was agreed that he was too old to take on the principal chieftainship of a troubled tribe.

White Bear, about 45, was a more likely choice. In some ways he was like Little Mountain: a capable man, jovial and outgoing, a noted warrior—but more complex and flamboyant. For important occasions, such

Meeting with government delegates at Medicine Lodge Creek, Kansas, in 1867, Kiowa dignitaries reluctantly accept a plan to concentrate the tribe on a reservation in Indian Territory—later Oklahoma. If the Indians had not acquiesced, the government intended to "conquer a peace."

Seeking a site for a military post on the new reservation shared by Kiowas and Comanches, Army scouts arrive at Medicine Bluff Creek in southwestern Indian Territory—a locale where warriors held religious vigils. Fort Sill was established nearby in 1869.

42

An era of fierce suzerainty over the southern plains came to an end in 1875 as these Kiowa, Comanche, Cheyenne and Arapaho militants arrived in St. Augustine, Florida, sentenced to an indefinite stay in a military prison 1,000 miles from their homeland.

Tired of trying to elude the Army after leaving the reservation, a band of Kiowa raiders surrenders near Fort Sill in 1875.

Record of a bitter journey into exile

On April 28, 1875, 72 Kiowas and allied tribesmen—identified as ringleaders in recent raids against whites—looked upon their families at Fort Sill for what they thought would be the last time. Then, guarded by troops, they set forth on a 24-day journey by wagon and railroad to Fort Marion, a decaying, Spanish-built strong point in St. Augustine, Florida.

They expected to be executed there. Instead, they learned that their sentence was indefinite imprisonment. The difference seemed slight—until they became acquainted with the Army officer who was in charge of them. Lieutenant Richard Henry Pratt was like no white soldier in their experience. Although he had fought against the Kiowas, he perceived that the task at hand was to educate, not punish.

Pratt quickly had the Indians moved out of Fort Marion's humid dungeons and into barracks they built themselves. He put them to work as bakers, sailors, fishermen and field laborers—for pay —and he enlisted the help of white women to teach them to read and write English. Nor did he insist that they forswear their past entirely. With his encouragement, the younger warriors began to draw pictures narrating and explaining Indian life. One young Kiowa named Zotom chose a subject of particular immediacy—the deportation to Florida, shown here and on the following pages.

Three years after the Kiowa exile began, Pratt persuaded his superiors that the prisoners were firmly converted to the white man's road, and they were granted freedom. Most returned to the reservation, but a few of the once-fierce raiders chose to stay in the East. Wrote one: "I good boy now."

As a guard detachment stands by, authorities at Fort Sill ask the defeated Indians the identity of their war leaders. There was much covering up. Only the most notorious raiders were named for deportation and some deportees were later found to be obscure tribesmen or Mexican captives.

At a campsite on the way to the railroad that would take them to Fort Marion, the prisoners bathe in the Blue River in Indian Territory. The tents were reserved for their 4th Cavalry escort; the warriors were forced to sleep on the bare ground, shackled together with a continuous chain.

An excited crowd gathers at the Indianapolis railroad station to gawk at the warriors — a scene repeated in every city along the way. Riding on a train terrified the Indians, and some kept their blankets over their heads. Near the journey's end, one chief was shot to death attempting to escape.

52

The day after reaching St. Augustine, the Indians are brought to the parapet of Fort Marion to view the Atlantic Ocean. During the first few weeks of confinement in sweltering cells that lacked exterior windows, one warrior died of natural causes and a chief starved himself to death.

Fantastic rock formations in the Dragoon Mountains of southeastern Arizona conceal the entranceway to a narrow, six-mile-long canyon — the only access to a 40-acre valley where Cochise's Chiricahua warriors could find water, grass and near-perfect security after one of their raids.

A warrior finds a receptive audience as he spins out a tale, using a stick as a narrative aid. Storytelling was a favorite pastime of the Indians; many of their yarns were in praise of tribesmen who excelled in the Apache virtues of stealing without being caught and killing without being killed.

Only a few months of the traditional life of hunting and raiding remained to Geronimo's renegade group when this picture was taken during an unsuccessful peace parley in 1886. Several warriors wear the distinctive Apache boot, which could be pulled over the knee as protection against cactus.

COSTUMES MEXICAINS.
Cacique Apache
des bords du Rio Colorado dans la Californie.

Apache warlords: Cochise and Geronimo

One spring shortly before the midpoint of the 19th Century (the exact year remains uncertain) the leaders of the Mimbres Apache band assembled in council to consider their future dealings with the Mexican state of Chihuahua, which lay on the southern fringe of their traditional range. Included in the council was a young warrior named Gokhlayeh (One Who Yawns). Although he was entitled to speak his mind, his opinions were not likely to carry much weight; he was still in his twenties and not yet a man of much importance in a group dominated by the great chief, Mangas Coloradas. But a decision reached at the meeting proved fateful for Gokhlayeh. The chain of events begun that day would ultimately earn him a new identity that became a war cry recognized all over the world: Geronimo. Along with his fellow Apache, Cochise, the man known as Geronimo would be responsible for some of the bloodiest, bitterest and most unremitting fighting ever waged by Indian against white.

Ironically, the issue at hand was whether or not to accept a peace bribe. For 200 years, the Apaches had preyed on the villages, the haciendas, the herds and pack trains of Mexico; in return, they were warred upon by Mexican soldiery. In no man's memory had there been a time when Mexicans and Apaches had not hated each other. To the Mexicans, the Apaches were a scourge and a curse. To the pragmatic Apaches, the Mexicans, once assigned the role of unwilling suppliers, were worthy of nothing but contempt. Even so, the Indians did not scorn taking Mexican women — if comely — as wives to bear and rear sons who would kill more Mexican men. (Mangas Coloradas, whose name was Spanish for Red Sleeves, himself had a Mexican wife.)

Now the government of Chihuahua was willing to give up bloodlessly what the Apaches would otherwise have seized in violence. In one of their rare peaceful contacts with the Indians, the Mexicans let it be known that, at certain stations four times a year, the Apaches would be welcomed and issued supplies of blankets, cloth, meal and other necessities — and mescal, the fiery distilled essence of the agave plant, for which Apache men suffered a powerful thirst.

This was indeed a tempting proposition. Nevertheless, the Apaches were under no illusion that genuine brotherhood waited in Chihuahua. Since 1837, the state had been paying a bounty of 100 pesos for a male Apache scalp, 50 for a woman's, 25 for a child's. Although Chihuahua was now offering to suspend the bounty system, deep animosities surely lingered. Perhaps killing was a habit too deeply rooted to be easily changed by government order. In any case, the Apaches knew that whatever Chihuahua did, the adjoining state of Sonora would continue to pay scalp money.

After weighing the dangers against the potential gains, Mangas Coloradas recommended that a party set forth to receive the tribute, and most of the other men at the council agreed with him. Gokhlayeh was free to stand aloof, for no Apache warrior owed blind allegiance to a chief. He decided to go. It was an important venture for his people — and possibly it would present opportunities to assert himself as a leader.

If Gokhlayeh sometimes felt that he had a greater right than most men to a role of leadership, that was only natural. Chieftainship was hereditary among the Apaches, and his grandfather had been the chief of the Nedni Apaches, a band that roved the wilds of northern Mexico. However, his father had forfeited his — and his future son's — inheritance when he left his own peo-

An Apache chief, as envisioned by Italian artist Claudio Linati in 1828, conjures up the image of Genghis Khan. Linati was attempting to interpret the Apaches' legendary ferocity for a book about Mexico.

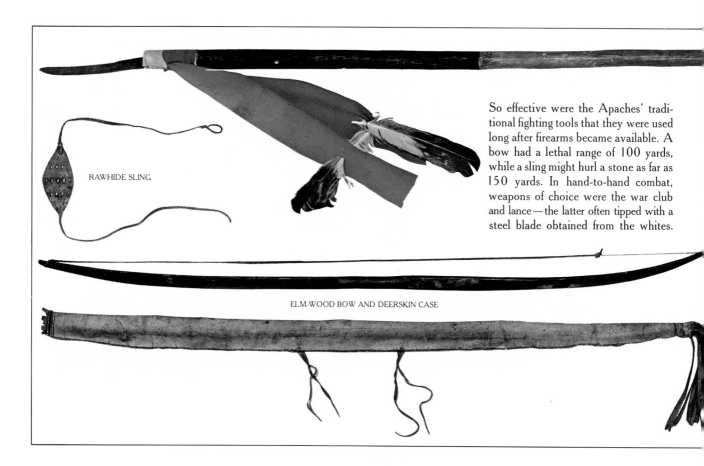

RAWHIDE SLING

So effective were the Apaches' traditional fighting tools that they were used long after firearms became available. A bow had a lethal range of 100 yards, while a sling might hurl a stone as far as 150 yards. In hand-to-hand combat, weapons of choice were the war club and lance—the latter often tipped with a steel blade obtained from the whites.

ELM-WOOD BOW AND DEERSKIN CASE

ple to marry into the Mimbres. Thus Gokhlayeh's ambitions were focused on a second route to prestige —through war and pillage. By showing himself to be an exceptional fighter, he might win respect equaling or even surpassing that of a hereditary chief. And that would be honor indeed, for the Apaches could not conceive of a people more powerful than themselves.

At a time faded from memory they had come into this land as conquerors. Speaking a dialect of the Athapascan tongue, once heard all across the northwestern part of the continent, they first appeared in the north of what would become New Mexico and Arizona. They pushed onto the Mogollon Rim, that gigantic upthrust of rock bearing the mighty canyon scar of the Colorado River. From the rim they looked southward across the hot desert waste toward the majestic peaks of the Sierra Madre in Mexico.

All this became theirs. Moving against the cliff-dwelling Zunis in the center, the Comanches to the east and the Yumans to the west, the invaders carved

out a range that measured 500 miles across and as much north to south. Here, sheltering in frail hovels of sticks and brush called wickiups, they lived as nomadic hunters, uninterested in farming except for an occasional garden patch of maize.

The vast territory was divided among a loose-knit confederation of bands that mostly went their separate ways and sometimes even warred on one another. But if their unity was tenuous, the various peoples with whom they came in conflict saw them as a single foe. Indeed the name Apache was apparently derived from the Zuni word *apachu,* "enemy." Passed on to Spaniard, to Mexican, to American, the word never lost its validity. Each successive pretender to the Apaches' terrain discovered them to be an antagonist who expected and gave no quarter.

Gokhlayeh, like every Apache male, had been drilled from boyhood in the cardinal virtues of cunning and toughness—the twin sources of his people's strength. He was taught that trickery ranked above pure courage:

64

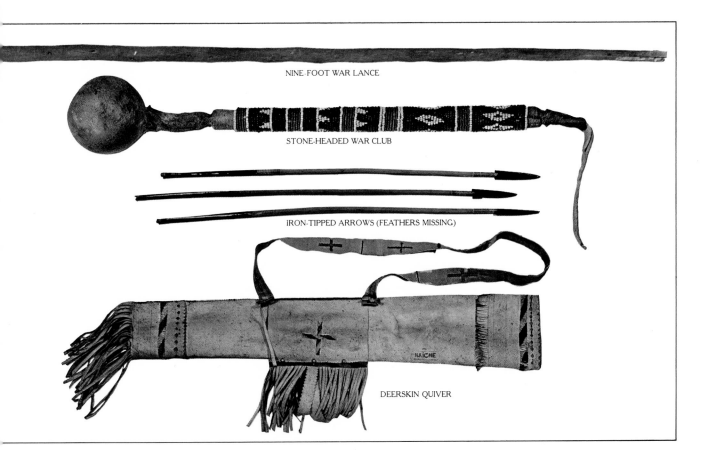

NINE-FOOT WAR LANCE

STONE-HEADED WAR CLUB

IRON-TIPPED ARROWS (FEATHERS MISSING)

DEERSKIN QUIVER

raiders who could quietly make off with a few horses or cattle from a Mexican ranch were more esteemed than those who won a bigger haul but suffered losses in the process. He was made to stay awake for long periods to learn how to deal with exhaustion. He trained as a long-distance runner, traversing four-mile courses through rough country, carrying a mouthful of water all the way without swallowing it or spitting it out. (A mature Apache warrior had to be able to cover 70 miles a day on foot, in the most forbidding terrain.) With arrows or rocks flung from slings, he fought scarcely mock battles against other acolytes. To survive, the boys relied only on hide shields and agility.

Out of such strenuous apprenticeship emerged a youth who was uniquely equipped to fight or flee in his environment of desert, mesquite, grassy valley or crag and canyon. By the time of the conference on Chihuahua's tempting offer, Gokhlayeh had been well blooded. He had grown to be a man of medium height —five feet seven inches or so—big chested, with a fierce

countenance of overhung brows, outthrust cheekbones, and a hawk's-beak nose above a straight, thin mouth. Later one of his eight battle wounds caused the right corner of his mouth to droop in a permanent sneer.

At that council to consider the Chihuahua offer, it was decided to include women and children in the peace party, for women would be needed as burden bearers to fetch home the tribute. Gokhlayeh took his young wife, Alope, their three young children and his aged mother. The party moved out of the Apache stronghold in the Mogollon Mountains in the southwestern portion of present-day New Mexico and started south. Their destination, the distribution point for tribute, was the village of Janos, about 60 miles into Mexico, in the foothills of the Sierra Madre.

The Apache party had no way of knowing that a man as warlike as themselves also had Janos much on his mind. He was the military governor of Sonora, General José Maria Carrasco. Several years later, Carrasco met Major John Cremony of the U.S. Army—then engaged in surveying the Mexican-American border—and related that he had been aware of the impending peace bribe and had resented it. "Not being able to comprehend the virtues of a policy which feeds Indians in one state that they might prey upon and destroy the citizens of another, I concluded that it was my duty to destroy the enemy wherever I could find him," he said. And so, while Gokhlayeh and his fellow tribesmen moved southward toward Chihuahua, General Carrasco, with two troops of Mexican cavalry, moved eastward from Sonora by forced night marches, heading for the same place.

The Indians arrived at Janos first. With inbred caution, they pitched their main camp well outside the town. Against the possibility of trouble, they also chose a rendezvous area in protective thickets beside the Janos River. Then the headmen and a few warriors approached the town to test the temperature of their welcome. Their reception was as open-handed and guileless as they could have wished, and they returned to camp laden with blankets, bright cloth, trade trinkets and armloads of bottled goods. That night there was feasting and a grand spree. The second day was even better, and the warriors detailed to remain and guard the camp were solaced by drink.

General Carrasco's cavalry struck on the third day. The blow was swift and merciless. The general withheld the order to open fire until the camp was entirely surrounded. The first volley cut down women over the cooking fires, killed infants at the breast, killed warriors sleeping off a hangover. Then Carrasco's men charged with club and bayonet. In a few minutes, the screams and moans died away as the cavalrymen finished off the wounded. The few survivors who had bolted through the Mexican lines crept into the brush. "We killed 130 and took about 90 prisoners, principally women and children," General Carrasco was to tell Major Cremony, adding in annoyed tones: "Colonel Medina, commanding the state of Chihuahua, was so enraged at my action that he made formal complaint to the Supreme Government which, however, after some unnecessary delay, approved of my course."

Mangas Coloradas and Gokhlayeh were among the warriors who, returning at dusk after collecting tribute, were met and warned by fugitive survivors. Slowly the remnants of the group assembled at the rendezvous.

Scouts were sent to spy on the ruined camp, and when they reported the place completely occupied by Mexicans, the Apaches knew they could not retrieve their dead or try to rescue the captives. They counted those who had reached the rendezvous. Gokhlayeh's wife, mother and children were not present.

The murder of his family affected Gokhlayeh deeply. When he and the other survivors slipped back across the border and into their mountain fastness a few days later, Gokhlayeh gave in to intense grief. Tribal custom called for him to mourn his wife by burning her possessions; but he went further, burning his wickiup and the toys of his children as well. Fellow tribesmen began to discern profound changes in him. They had known him to be an affectionate husband and indulgent father, but now he turned bitter, quarrelsome and prone to unpredictable outbursts of wild violence. Many warriors came to fear and dislike him.

Over the next year, the Mimbres gradually recovered strength, fashioning new bows, lances and war clubs, and augmenting these weapons with a few guns taken in raids. Meanwhile, Gokhlayeh's lust for Mexican blood grew almost obsessive. And so it was a particular joy to him when Mangas Coloradas decided the time had come to summon a council to consider revenge. Mangas Coloradas was a giant among the Apaches, both figuratively and in body; he stood six feet, six inches tall, and he was brilliant. Just a few years earlier the Mexican government had mobilized fully 1,000 soldiers in a futile effort to run him down. Now he was almost 60, but his reputation for ferocity in war was undiminished.

The Mimbres chief decided that Gokhlayeh was the proper messenger to recruit warriors from other Apache bands. He was sent first to Cochise of the Chiricahuas. Commissioning a man of Gokhlayeh's modest attainments to approach Cochise as an equal was a signal honor for the former, almost an impertinence toward the latter. Cochise was recognized by all the scattered Apaches as a chief of Mangas Coloradas' caliber. Only a few years older than Gokhlayeh, Cochise had inherited from his father the leadership of the Chiricahuas, who commanded the region of the Dragoon and Chiricahua mountains in southeastern Arizona. Building on this legacy, he proved himself shrewd in war, sagacious in council, and deeply concerned for his people's welfare—all the qualities that evoked Apache loyalty.

As the Americans came to know him, they agreed in many ways with the Indian estimate of Cochise. Although they learned to fear him and tried hard to kill him, they recognized that he was a leader of rare presence and poise. Captain John Gregory Bourke, who at different times both pursued and talked peace with him, wrote: "Cochise is a fine-looking Indian, straight as a rush—six feet in stature, deep-chested and roman-nosed. A kindly and even somewhat melancholy expression tempers the determined look of his countenance. There was neither in speech or action any of the bluster characteristic of his race." (By contrast, Bourke would later say of Gokhlayeh: "He and his warriors were certainly as fine-looking a lot of pirates as ever cut a throat or scuttled a ship.")

Cochise consenting, Gokhlayeh addressed the Chiricahuas. "Kinsmen," Gokhlayeh told them, according to his own later account, "you have heard what the Mexicans have done without cause. We are men the same as the Mexicans are—we can do to them what they have done to us. Let us go forward—we will attack them in their homes. Will you come? It is well—you will all come."

With the Chiricahua agreement in hand, Gokhlayeh next was sent into the Sierra Madre to make contact with his father's original people, the Nednis, now under Chief Juh. They, too, agreed to join in the chastisement of Mexico. The chiefs chose as a target the rich agricultural town of Arizpe in Sonora, 120 miles south of Tucson. Arizpe was selected for sound strategic reasons. It was situated at the head of a narrow canyon, it would be difficult to reinforce, and the escape route back home lay through thinly populated farmland.

In the summer of the year following the massacre at Janos, a great war party gathered and, as the sun set, began a nightlong war dance around a huge bonfire. To the throb of drums and the chanting of seated warriors, four dancers came out abreast, circled the fire four times, separated into pairs and danced south and north of the flames. Four times more they repeated the routine. (The number four and the cardinal points of the compass were sacred to the Apaches and found a place in most tribal rituals.) As the drums beat on, the moment came for individuals to declare their intention. A warrior who pledged to fight could signify the fact merely by walking around the fire; the more demonstrative leaped forward and, with prancing legs and gesticulating arms, enacted the ways in which they would kill. At dawn, the dance ended and the war party moved out afoot. It was no time to be encumbered by animals.

The Apaches made their final approach from the east, coming down through precipitous defiles of the Sierra Madre. Just outside Arizpe and across the Sonora River, the warriors—carefully staying out of sight—arrayed themselves in a great half circle, with the open side toward the town. Then a few of them moved into the open and waited for Arizpe to react. Response came quickly; eight horsemen bearing a flag of truce crossed the river, entered the semicircle and approached the handful of visible warriors. When they came within reach, more Apaches leaped from their concealed positions and killed them, leaving Arizpe in no doubt of its peril. In full view of the frightened town, the Indians scalped these first dead, a gesture to remind the Mexicans of their own scalp-bounty system.

At last a Mexican commander marched out on the attack with two companies of infantry, bringing along a pack train laden with ammunition and rations. In vengeful joy, Gokhlayeh believed he recognized the soldiers as the same unit that had killed his family. The fighting lasted all that first day. The Indians kept covetous eyes on the mule train and its valuable packs, realizing that, if they could seize it, they would be greatly strengthened. Just at dusk, they saw their chance. A sudden swoop out of the concealed flank and the train was in their hands. Dismayed, the Mexicans pulled back to the barricaded town.

The next morning the Mexican commander came out with his entire force, the infantry now backed by two cavalry companies. The Indians waited until the soldiers were within the semicircle and then charged. The Mexican line broke and the battle fell into wild confusion. Now the fighting was all over the field, without order on either side—bayonet against lance, saber against war club.

Gokhlayeh was everywhere—reckless, almost berserk. Probably he did not know how many men he killed that day; long afterward he was to say that Mexicans "were not worth counting. We kill Mexicans with rocks." Before the day ended he ceased to be Gokhlayeh. Somewhere in the melee, watching him in

Inheriting a leadership role because of his parental training, Mangas became chief of the Mimbres Apaches in 1863, when his father, Mangas Coloradas, died. However, since he never matched his father's prowess in battle, he was not as influential.

awe, an unknown Mexican, for an unknown reason, shouted "Geronimo!" Others took up the cry and ever after, to Indian and white alike, Gokhlayeh was Geronimo. The connotation is beyond explaining; in Spanish the word is the equivalent of "Jerome."

When the two sides separated after three hours of fighting, the field was littered with far more Mexican dead than Apache. Six men still held the field: Geronimo, three other Indians and two Mexican cavalrymen. The Mexicans fired, bringing down two of the warriors. Geronimo and the other Apache, weaponless except for knives in the leggings of their moccasins, sprinted for their own lines. One Mexican with a saber caught up with and brought down Geronimo's last companion. Geronimo ran on, seized a lance from another Apache, then turned back and killed his pursuer. Taking the slain man's saber, he went for the remaining Mexican. They grappled and fell. As they struggled, Geronimo dropped the saber, got one hand on the haft of his knife and killed his last enemy of the day.

Laden with booty and honor, blood lust requited, the war party moved back across the border. Gokhlayeh had been a man of minor consequence; nobody could say the same of Geronimo, then or thereafter.

But his hour of greatest renown—such as it was—still lay far in the future. For the moment, he left the Mimbres band, took a Chiricahua wife, and placed himself under the leadership of Cochise. It proved a satisfactory shift to a man who lived to wage war on whites, for Cochise was destined to become to the Americans what Mangas Coloradas was to the Mexicans: a source of dread.

The United States took over Mexico's claim to much of the Apaches' range by the Treaty of Guadalupe Hidalgo, which formally concluded the war between the two nations in 1846, and by the Gadsden Purchase of 1853, a $10 million transaction involving some 30,000 square miles of land south of the Gila River. At first, the new claimants seemed uninterested in occupying the land, aside from establishing a handful of mining outposts in Mangas Coloradas' territory during the mid-1850s. They didn't bother the old chief; he was willing to tolerate a few prospectors.

Cochise faced a more significant incursion in 1858 when the route for a transcontinental stage line, the But-

After both Cochise and his oldest son died within a two-year period, Naiche, the second son, succeeded to the position of chief of the Chiricahuas in 1876. But he had to share his power with a commoner who had a more riveting personality, Geronimo.

terfield Overland, was laid out across his land. In the heart of his stronghold he commanded a strategic passage and fresh water springs at Apache Pass, between the Dragoon and Chiricahua mountains. However, when Butterfield representatives sought permission to build a stage station there, Cochise granted it, realizing that useful knowledge might be gained from the newcomers. He stipulated only that the buildings must stand back several hundred yards from the springs, a precaution to ensure that these new neighbors, should they take such a notion, could not monopolize the precious water. By 1860 he was on terms good enough to negotiate what was probably the first formal commercial deal ever made by an Apache: a contract to cut firewood for the station.

But these fragile beginnings of friendship were soon shattered. At the time the firewood agreement was concluded, a ne'er-do-well white man, John Ward, was living with his mistress, a Mexican woman named Jesusa Martinez, on a nondescript ranch near the new Fort Buchanan, west of Apache Pass. With them was Felix, their 10- or 11-year-old son. During the summer some warriors of the Pinal Apache band raided the Ward place, drove off some cattle and abducted young Felix.

Ward reported the kidnapping to Fort Buchanan, but the fort was shorthanded and for months nothing was done. Meanwhile, Ward somehow conceived the notion (now known to be mistaken) that the kidnappers must be Cochise's men. The Army accepted his view. In January 1861, George N. Bascom, a young second lieutenant fresh to the West and eager to make a name, was dispatched to Apache Pass with 54 men — and Ward. At the stage station, Bascom paused long enough to plant a falsehood with James Wallace, a driver and personal friend of the Chiricahua leader. The soldiers, said the officer, were on a routine patrol toward the Rio Grande; then he continued on his way and camped in the canyon nearby.

Cochise soon appeared at the station and inquired about the intentions of such a large body of troops. Reassured, he decided to pay a formal call on the Army detachment. He took along his brother Naretena, his wife Nahlekadeya, his young son Nachise, and two warrior nephews. At the camp, the Apaches were bidden to enter Bascom's tent. When they sat down for polite dis-

Adorned with health symbols, the yard-high painting was done in vegetable dyes on doeskin.

A warrior's portrayal of a puberty dance

Like other Indians of the West, the Apaches were a deeply religious people who constantly propitiated the spirits believed to dwell everywhere in the natural world. Most of their ceremonies were private affairs. For instance, a warrior would sing a prayer over his weapons to strengthen them against the enemy (Geronimo was said to have a powerful rite of this kind).

Of the few public ceremonies, the most important was staged when a girl attained puberty. Scattered members of a band came together to thank the spirits for seeing her safe to child-bearing age and, by extension, for looking after their future. Thus when Naiche, a son of Cochise, decided in the 1890s to depict Apache customs, he chose this joyous ritual as his subject.

In the painting, shown in its entirety above and with its center enlarged at right, tribesmen dance facing a ceremonial fire, while seven girls — each paired under a blanket with an older woman who acted as a protector — dance off to the sides. They are joined by four masked warriors (top) wearing bizarre headdresses that identify them as mountain spirits, and by two small boys, serving as messengers between performers and onlookers (bottom). The ceremony lasted more than four days and its completion marked the promise of prosperity and long life.

Custom called for every girl to be so honored. But when the Apaches were placed on reservations, their white supervisors decided the rites were too time-consuming. They decreed that all the girls who came of age each year had to receive a single ceremony — to be held at the time the Americans were celebrating the Fourth of July.

To pass the time on the reservation, Apache men try their hand at an ancient betting game in which a pole was thrust at a rolling hoop.

Met by a cavalry officer and stray dogs, Apache women return from their hay-gathering labors.

A chair, factory-made pails and a canvas-sided wickiup mark a family's acceptance of alien ways.

VICTORIO

NANA

LOCO

CHATO

ALCHESAY

ESKAMINZIN

Apache proponents of peace and war

VICTORIO, who won a leadership role among the Mimbres by ability rather than birth, urged peace until the Army moved his people from a reservation on their original New Mexico lands to bleak San Carlos in 1877. Turning renegade, he led 250 warriors on a rampage that left 400 whites dead before he was killed in 1880.

NANA moved to the forefront of the remaining Mimbres renegades after the death of Victorio and held to the warpath, although he was rheumatic and in his seventies. With hundreds of soldiers in hot pursuit, his group of 40 warriors claimed more than 30 lives in less than two months. He later threw in his lot with Geronimo.

LOCO, an eloquent and widely respected voice for moderation among the Mimbres, was forced at gunpoint by Geronimo to leave the San Carlos reservation in 1882 and join the war on whites. Although he broke away and surrendered the next year, he was placed under military arrest and sent off to a prison in Florida.

CHATO was allied with Geronimo for a time but reformed in 1884 and became an Army scout. In 1886, he received a medal for services against Geronimo; then — just a few days later — the military, under pressure from nervous Arizonans, shipped him to Florida to be confined with the renegades he had helped bring to bay.

ALCHESAY, a chief of the White Mountain Apaches of eastern Arizona, never deviated from the path of friendship with the whites. He proved a peerless scout, received the Congressional Medal of Honor for valor in General George Crook's 1872-1873 campaign in Arizona, and went on to become a prominent cattleman.

ESKAMINZIN, chief of the Aravaipa Apaches of south-central Arizona, favored peace until 1871, when 144 of his people were massacred by Tucson vigilantes avenging raids by other Apaches. He shot his closest white friend, served a jail sentence and became a successful reservation farmer — until some miners took his land.

an eye like an eagle. He respected me; I respected him. He was a man who scorned a liar." A year later, this unlikely friendship would serve to defuse the foremost Apache enemy of the United States.

The end was almost anticlimactic. In 1872, President Grant sent a pious, one-armed Civil War officer to make peace with the Apaches. General Oliver O. Howard sought out Jeffords and asked to be led to the Chiricahua leader. When Cochise and Howard met in the mountains, the onlooking warriors were startled at the general's habit in moments of importance of suddenly dropping on one knee to pray. Assured by Jeffords that Howard was consulting the Almighty and not making bad medicine, they relaxed.

Cochise and Howard spent 11 days in negotiations and finally settled their differences. The Chiricahuas were allowed to keep their weapons, their way of life and their own traditional range; they were granted a reservation that enclosed the Chiricahua and Dragoon mountains where they had lived, hunted and fought time out of mind. At Cochise's insistence, Jeffords was appointed reservation agent. And at Jeffords' insistence, the Interior Department granted the new agent absolute authority to deal with the Chiricahuas and to keep away any white intruder, civilian or military.

"The white man and the Indian are to drink of the same water, eat of the same bread and be at peace," Cochise said when the pact was sealed. He was not privileged to enjoy this new era of coexistence for long. In 1874, in his fifty-first year, he was taken mortally ill. Near the end, he called Jeffords to his blanket.

"Brother, do you think you will ever see me alive again?" Cochise asked.

"No," Jeffords replied, "I think by tomorrow night you will be dead."

"Yes, I think so — about 10 o'clock tomorrow morning. Do you think we will ever meet again?"

"I don't know," Jeffords confessed. "What is your opinion?"

"I believe good friends will meet somewhere," Cochise said.

The chief was dead by the hour he named. That night his warriors painted him in yellow, black and vermilion, shrouded him in a red blanket, propped him on his favorite horse and took him deep into the mountains. They lowered his body and his weapons into a crevice whose location was never afterward revealed.

For two years after the death of Cochise, Jeffords managed to maintain a semblance of peace. But with Cochise gone his task was not easy. Gradually the situation began to slip out of his control. Increasing numbers of warriors, following Geronimo's lead, used the reservation merely as a sanctuary: they raided in Mexico and returned when things got too hot. Often these vacationing marauders brought stolen horses and cattle with them to sell to reservation brethren.

Mexican authorities complained to Jeffords bitterly, and in 1876 Americans, too, gained cause for deep grievance. That March, two stagecoach attendants on the reservation heard that some raiders had returned from Mexico with stolen gold and silver; to get their hands on some of the loot they offered to sell the Apaches whiskey at the equivalent of $10 a bottle. The warriors, swapping booty for booze, became drunk. Soon the liquor was gone and the Indians demanded more. When they were refused, they killed both white men. The next day, continuing their murderous binge, they killed a rancher in the vicinity. Jeffords called in the Army and tracked the offenders into the Dragoon Mountains, but he failed to capture them.

The outcry among Arizonans was immediate and vehement. Governor Anson P. Safford demanded that Washington replace Jeffords. The *Arizona Citizen* of Tucson declared in mid-April: "The kind of war needed for the Chiricahua Apaches is steady, unrelenting, hopeless, and undiscriminating war, slaying men, women and children, until every valley and crest and crag and fastness shall send to high heaven the grateful incense of festering and rotting Chiricahuas."

Washington responded by dissolving the Chiricahua reservation in June 1876 and removing the band — or as many of its members as could be found — to San Carlos, the largest reservation in the Southwest, shared by some 4,000 other Apaches. However, Geronimo, learning of the plan, hastened across the border, along with his family and other recalcitrant Chiricahuas.

In the years to come, Geronimo would earn himself a conspicuous place in Western history as the ultimate holdout, a renegade who was willing to fight for his freedom and the traditional way of life longer and more ferociously than any other Apache leader — or almost any other Indian, for that matter. Although the largest group he ever led numbered a mere 100 followers, he was credited with possessing a fiery, unyielding spirit that no man could break.

Legend oversimplified him. Geronimo was, in fact, something of a paradox: alternately tough-minded and indecisive; a man who sometimes stayed and fought, sometimes cut and ran; a chief who interrupted his career as a holdout to test reservation life, never finding it quite to his taste, but never deciding against it altogether. To the end, he seemed a prisoner of the per-sonality that had emerged after his wife was murdered at Janos long before, given to passions that inspired fear, awe and horror — but that somehow never amounted to more than a mystery.

His first stint as a holdout was short-lived. Late in the winter of 1876-1877, he came out of Mexico into the vicinity of the Warm Springs agency in New Mexico, where the Mimbres Apaches resided. Geronimo's visit was not merely social: he had a herd of stolen cattle to trade or sell. Weeks later, news of his where-abouts reached the agent of San Carlos, a cocky young

Never one to shun publicity, Geronimo (in front of horse) lines up his warriors for a Tombstone photographer who crossed the Mexican border to

man named John Clum, who immediately set off on the 400-mile journey to Warm Springs to apprehend him.

In April, Geronimo received word that Clum desired to talk. In no wise intimidated, Geronimo painted himself for war, took up his weapons, summoned a dozen of his leading warriors and rode three miles to the agency. He found Clum sitting on the veranda, surrounded by a half-dozen Indian police, with a few others standing nearby. The San Carlos agent opened proceedings on a characteristically imperious note: "No harm will come to you if you listen with good ears." Geronimo, noting Clum's small force, was not humbled. "Speak with discretion," he advised the agent, "and no harm will come to *you*." To emphasize the point, he hitched up the rifle in his arms.

At that moment, Clum touched the brim of his hat. It was a signal. The doors of an adjoining commissary building burst open and 80 additional policemen charged out and surrounded Geronimo's party with leveled guns. Geronimo began to thumb back the hammer of his rifle but thought better of it and stood motionless, stolidly watchful. Clum approached him. "I'll take

record peace negotiations with General Crook in 1886. At the time, the renegade group numbered 35 men and 80 women and children.

The departure of cavalry patrols from Fort Bowie was a familiar sight as long as Cochise and Geronimo were at large. The fortress was built in 1862 to control Apache Pass, a vital route through the Chiricahua Mountains that opened the way between Tucson and all points East.

Santiago McKinn *(foreground),* an Irish-Mexican lad captured by Geronimo, was freed during negotiations with General Crook. The boy's physical condition caused bitter controversy. Outwardly he seemed unharmed, but some in Crook's retinue insisted "his mind was almost ruined."

a dozen other leaders deliberately staged a spree with homemade beer, then openly admitted the deed — figuring that the authorities would hesitate to discipline so many prominent Indians. The ranking military officer at San Carlos, new to the job, composed a telegram to Crook, asking for instructions; however, before sending it, he showed it to his chief of scouts, a man named Al Sieber. As it happened, Sieber was badly hung over from a spree of his own; he mumbled that the problem did not amount to anything, and the inexperienced officer simply put the telegram aside.

Geronimo and the others grew increasingly apprehensive as they waited for some response from the authorities. The interminable delay seemed to bode ill, and finally, unable to bear the suspense, Geronimo decamped, taking along 42 men and 92 women and children. Before leaving, he sent his warriors to cut the telegraph wire, concealing this sabotage by making the cut in the crotch of a tree and tying the wire ends with a rawhide thong.

Collecting supplies on the way south, he attacked the ranch of a man named Phillips, killed him, his wife and an infant. He also hanged their five-year-old daughter on a meat hook. She was still alive when a posse arrived from Silver City, but died a few hours later.

Crook was furious when he learned about the unsent telegram. He later wrote, "I am firmly convinced that had I known of the occurrence, the outbreak would not have occurred." He mounted the heaviest campaign in the Apache wars up to that time, with 20 cavalry troops and more than 200 Indian scouts — 3,000 men in all. Once again, his policy of using scouts paid off, although more slowly this time, for Geronimo knew they were coming and was more cautious.

Throughout the winter of 1885-1886, Crook's forces hunted the foe in the Sierra Madre. In January, they surprised one camp and captured the renegades' horses and supplies, although their quarry escaped. Finally, in March, Geronimo's followers persuaded him to meet Crook a few miles south of the border.

When the general arrived, he did not find Geronimo or his men looking particularly discouraged. "Though tired of the constant hounding of the campaign," Crook later recalled, "they were in superb physical condition, armed to the teeth, fierce as so many tigers. Knowing what pitiless brutes they are themselves, they mistrust

The twilight years of a living legend

Geronimo, the most notorious of the Apache leaders, was about 57 years old but still a forbidding figure in 1886, when he surrendered and began a 23-year exile in Florida and Oklahoma. The portfolio of portraits here and on the following pages records his degeneration from a haughty warrior into a submissive old man who hawked pictures of himself in outlandish attire that no Chiricahua ever wore. Through it all, he nourished a forlorn hope. "I want to go back to my old home before I die," he confided to a reporter in 1908. It was not to be. The next year Geronimo died and was buried at Fort Sill, 700 miles from the crags and deserts where he had inspired such fear.

1886

1890

C. 1894

C. 1903

C. 1904

1905

His lance poised for the kill, a Comanche warrior overtakes an Osage in artist George Catlin's tribute to the master equestrians of the plains.

3 | Final champion of Comanche glory

In the late 1860s, a war chief of riveting appeal arose among the Comanches of the southern plains. He was a half-breed named Quanah; the Texans on whom he preyed would later call him Quanah Parker, after his white mother, Cynthia Ann Parker, who as a young girl had been captured by Comanches. Quanah's slashing raids and hairbreadth escapes from the U.S. cavalry rekindled war fever among the Plains Indians who were still free; and those who had already signed themselves over to a stagnant reservation existence thirsted after news of his exploits, hoping he might somehow reverse their fortunes.

His people were horsemen without peer. While many other Plains tribesmen rode to meet the enemy and then dismounted to fight, the Comanches always fought on horseback. They routinely traveled hundreds of miles to execute a lightning raid, and their prowess in battle made them prodigiously rich in captured animals: ordinary warriors often owned 250 horses, and chiefs like Quanah might have more than a thousand.

Not even Quanah and his spectacularly mobile warriors could long withstand the whites' overwhelming superiority in numbers, resources and organization. However, when the inevitable time for surrender arrived, he devoted himself to an even greater career — as a politician and financier who found ways to merge the interests of the two peoples whose blood flowed in his veins.

The two lives of Quanah Parker

In the early 1870s, it seemed to the whites that nothing but a fatal bullet could make a "good" Indian out of Quanah, the notorious half-breed Comanche chief. While the tribe's other war leaders were leading their defeated bands onto the Fort Sill reservation in Indian Territory, Quanah and his followers in the Kwahadi band kept up their murderous attacks on frontier settlements across nearly half of Texas. Cavalry Captain Robert Carter, a battle-scarred veteran of the Indian wars, described the Kwahadi horsemen as "the most inveterate raiders on the Texas border," and he blamed Quanah for "some of the foulest deeds ever recorded in the annals of Indian warfare."

Quanah fought with reckless, fanatic zeal. This much Carter learned at close hand one day in west Texas, when he and a detachment of troopers barely stood off a Kwahadi war party until help arrived from their main column two miles away. "A large and powerfully built chief led the bunch on a coal black racing pony," Carter wrote in his memoirs. "His heels nervously working in the animal's side, with six-shooter poised in air, he seemed the incarnation of savage brutal joy. His face was smeared with black war paint, which gave his features a satanic look. A large cruel mouth added to his ferocious appearance. Bells jingled as he rode at headlong speed, followed by the leading warriors, all eager to outstrip him in the race."

This demon on horseback was never truly vanquished in his many battles with the Army. Yet suddenly, in 1875, Quanah gave up his wars and his wanderings and accepted a cramped, sedentary reservation life. Moreover, the U.S. Congress later praised his public service in persuading his tribe to quit the warpath for good. Quanah was, in fact, an anomaly — a chief who was equally great in war and in the enforced peace that followed, when he emerged as an energetic and enlightened protector of his people's interests.

What caused Quanah's unlikely turnabout? Some Texans, grudging admirers of their tormentor, credited him with a statesman-like decision to save the remnants of his tribe, even though the price was his own surrender. Other Texans, aware that Quanah had been born to a white mother, figured that his white blood had somehow prompted a change of allegiance. The notion was absurd. Although Quanah seemed to lead two very different lives, he was wholly Comanche in both of them, never forswearing the heritage of a people who ranked as the greatest horse-warriors in the West.

The tribal world that shaped Quanah had begun to take shape itself sometime around the year 1700, when Comanche horsemen migrated southward from the Wyoming region. No tribe or alliance of tribes in their path could match their equestrian prowess, and by the middle of the 18th Century they had not only established themselves as reigning lords of the southern plains but had played a possibly momentous role in American history by blocking the northward expansion of the Spanish, holding the bulk of them in southern Texas.

The Comanches reached the peak of their power early in the 19th Century. They were then one of the largest Indian tribes, about 20,000 strong, occupying a range of some 240,000 square miles, mostly in Texas but also including adjacent areas of what would become Kansas, Colorado, New Mexico and Oklahoma. This enormous dominion was shared by five main Comanche bands, all completely autonomous and acknowledging no principal chief. The bands were free to carry on any war they pleased, except with fellow tribesmen. Their

Prior to tribal festivities in the 1890s, Comanche chief Quanah, his braids wrapped in beaver fur, wears traditional attire. By then a well-connected businessman, he was more likely to be seen in a suit and tie.

Hunters take their ease as women labor in a Comanche village visited by artist George Catlin in 1834. At that time, the 20,000 members of the powerful tribe controlled an enormous range centered in northwestern Texas and measuring 600 miles north to south, 400 miles east to west.

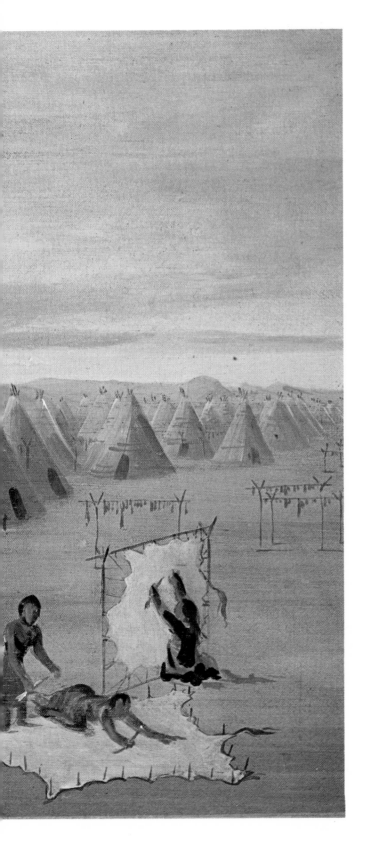

favorite targets were the outposts of New Spain—or Mexico, as the area was called after its citizens revolted against a distant monarchy in 1821. War parties sometimes thrust hundreds of miles into Mexico and returned with as many as 1,000 stolen horses.

The Spanish and Mexicans in Texas, never numbering more than a few thousand, were regarded as a feeble enemy by the Comanches. But the tribe faced a more daunting foe when Anglo-Americans began appearing in eastern Texas in the 1820s; they kept coming in such numbers that within a few years settlers were encroaching on the Indians' buffalo-hunting plains.

A long and venomous war between the newcomers and the Comanches began shortly after Texas won independence from Mexico early in 1836. In the first serious clash—an exhilarating victory for the Comanches—Quanah's mother, Cynthia Ann Parker, was taken captive. Cynthia Ann was then nine years old and living in Parker's Fort, a stockaded cluster of homesteads set up by her parents and kinfolk near the town of Groesbeck, in east-central Texas. When raiders attacked Parker's Fort, they set a pattern of savagery that both sides followed for decades thereafter. Grandfather Parker had his scalp taken and his genitals ripped off before he was killed. Grandmother Parker was pinned to the ground with a lance, stripped and allowed to live to suffer her pain and degradation.

Cynthia Ann was one of five white women and children abducted by the warriors. Like most young white captives, she adjusted readily to the Indian life and was adopted by the Comanches, who suffered from a low birth rate. In her teens, she became the wife of Peta Nocona, a rising young chief of the Noconas, one of the main bands. Early in her marriage, she gave birth to Quanah—meaning "fragrant" in Comanche. The infant looked just like a full-blooded Comanche, except that his eyes were blue-gray instead of black. As Quanah grew into a strong, tall boy, Cynthia Ann bore another son, Pecos, and a daughter, Prairie Flower.

Three children were a larger-than-average brood for a Comanche woman, and Nocona was so pleased with his productive blue-eyed spouse that, though most chiefs took several wives, he remained monogamous. Cynthia Ann was as content as her husband. In the 1850s, some white hunters met her on the plains and offered to pay ransom for her freedom. She refused, saying she

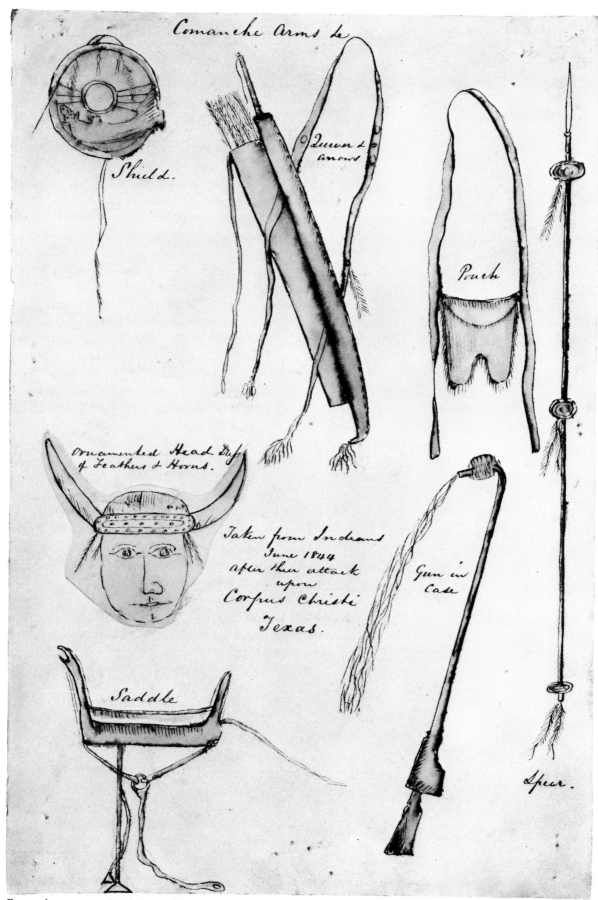

Comanche war gear, sketched by a British visitor to Texas, includes a pouch for charms that summoned divine aid in battle.

106

had children to care for and that she loved her husband.

Quanah, like all Comanche children, grew up on horseback. He learned to ride with his mother almost as soon as he could walk, and by the time he was five he had a pony of his own and was practicing with a small bow and blunt arrows as he rode at increasing speeds. A Comanche's boyhood was a pampered, sportive idyl, and from the time Quanah was nine or 10 he and other youths were taking midnight joy rides on the moonlit prairie, playing rough games and enviously watching the warriors parade around camp before leaving on raids. Quanah learned that Comanche men hunted to live, but lived to win honors and booty in war.

Because anyone who did not fight was not truly a man to the Comanches, many aging warriors felt that life had become purposeless, and they would bitterly quote the Comanche proverb, "A brave man dies young." More than a few elderly warriors, realizing that their skills and strength were fast slipping away, chose to commit suicide by battle. One such glorious death was witnessed—and abetted—by a troop of U.S. cavalry in 1860. The soldiers, pursuing a Comanche raiding party, saw an aged warrior dismount up ahead. He removed his moccasins, a sure sign that he did not intend to leave that spot alive. The old man fought hard and wounded three soldiers and their commanding officer before he died with more than 20 bullets in him. But while he made his brave stand, his friends were able to get away.

Quanah probably went on his first raid—and killed his first enemy—by the age of 15. The success of the mission was practically a foregone conclusion, in part because the Texas frontier was too extended to defend at all points against surprise attack, and also because Comanche raiders never neglected to plan for their retreat. If the target lay at any appreciable distance, they traveled with a change of horses in tow. The warriors would set up a temporary camp not far from the intended point of attack, and leave their spare horses there before swooping in for the kill. It took hours for any settler who escaped their scalping knives to round up a relief force, and the rescuers could not reach the ravaged settlement for hours more. By then the booty-laden warriors would have returned to their temporary camp, carefully traveling over rocky areas and through stream beds to conceal their tracks. Mounted on fresh horses, they would ride as much as 100 miles without stopping for food or rest. Even if they were tracked to their temporary camp and beyond, their pursuers stood only a slim chance of catching them.

Years before Quanah came of age, the Texans had learned that it was foolish to wait for Comanche raids and then launch vain pursuits; the best defense was to reply in kind, by surprise attack. In 1835, the Texans had established a small but tough militia, the Texas Rangers. The Rangers patrolled constantly to intercept raiding parties, and they probed deep into Comanche territory to strike vulnerable encampments.

When the Republic of Texas joined the United States in 1845, the Texans had every reason to expect the U.S. Army to take over their war with the Comanches. After the Mexican War of 1846, the Army did indeed begin building a string of forts across central Texas, but at first the posts were manned only by infantrymen, whose worth against the mobile Comanches was nil. The Texans were bitterly disappointed, but they soon got some unexpected help. In 1849, prospectors poured through Comanche territory on their way to the California gold fields, and they left a virulent cholera epidemic in their wake. Like their Kiowa allies, every Comanche band suffered heavy casualties, and the largest band, the Penatekas, lost about half of its population. In late 1854, many of the Penatekas surrendered and were consigned to a reservation on the Clear Fork of the Brazos River in north-central Texas. The other Comanche bands were able to hold out all through the 1850s, although the Texas Rangers, along with the U.S. cavalry, continued to exact a steady toll by surprise attacks. One such attack in December 1860 brought disaster upon Quanah's band.

The Noconas were confidently camped near the Pease River, with most of the men off hunting buffalo and the women drying meat for their winter food supply, when a force of 40 Texas Rangers and 21 U.S. cavalrymen—all under the command of Ranger Captain Sul Ross—suddenly struck, killing a number of Indians and taking several captives. After the battle, it was noticed that one of the women had Caucasian features and blue eyes. Even though she spoke no English, her captors suspected that she was Cynthia Ann Parker, known to be living among the Comanches. They summoned her Uncle Isaac, and he positively identified her

In the original illustrations of her narrative, Mrs. Harris grieves for her murdered husband before being dragged into the dwelling of a Comanche.

A white woman's ordeal as a Comanche captive

In raids against their traditional Spanish and Mexican enemies, Comanches frequently abducted young women for marriage — a practice they justified by the need to overcome their low birth rate. Texas settlers got their first taste of this aspect of war in the summer of 1835 — almost a year before the seizure of the girl who would become Quanah's mother — when Comanche marauders ambushed a pair of emigrant families, sparing only two women. One of them later provided a vivid, if stilted, account of her ordeal in a book, *History of the Captivity and Providential Release Therefrom of Mrs. Caroline Harris.*

She and Mrs. Clarissa Plummer were taken by the Indians to a distant village where two young chiefs drew lots for them. Mrs. Harris, her body daubed with red dye, found herself the reluctant bride at "a mock ceremony uniting me to the ruthless savage whose companion I was to become." Resistance, she realized, would only have subjected her "to all the tortures that their inventive faculties could have given birth to."

Life in a Comanche tipi proved to hold more drudgery than terror. "The savage treated me as his menial servant while his own time was employed in fishing, the chase and other amusements," wrote Mrs. Harris. She also complained of the chief's inebriated homecomings: "My only safety was in flight to some neighboring swamp until he became sober."

But if she found nothing agreeable about being a chief's wife, the Comanche seemed pleased enough with the arrangement. On one occasion he led a search party that found Mrs. Harris after she had been lost in a forest for three days. "An uncommon degree of joy and satisfaction was manifested by my Indian companion," she recalled, quickly adding, "but whether it was to be imputed to genuine love, or the high value he set upon me, I never knew."

Her use of the word value was not figurative. In 1837, a white hunter, having learned of her fate, paid the Comanches a ransom of $400 and brought the two-year travail to an end.

as his niece, lost 24 years earlier. He took her and young Prairie Flower back to east Texas to live with the Parker clan.

Quanah's reaction to the recapture of his mother can only be guessed at in light of his persistent later efforts to learn of her fate. Obviously he loved Cynthia Ann, and an adolescent boy — even a fierce Comanche — was bound to be shaken by the sudden loss of a parent. Almost certainly, the loss added an urge for vengeance to his hatred for the whites who kept proclaiming themselves the masters of the Comanche range.

Quanah suffered other losses in quick succession. His father died, reportedly of an infected wound, and his brother Pecos then died of disease. With no one left to hold him in the Nocona band, Quanah joined the powerful Kwahadies, a band that lived on the edge of the Staked Plains of west Texas, a timberless tableland bordered by steep escarpments; the region's name recalled an early Spanish surveying venture.

Among the Comanches, individual warriors and whole families changed bands freely, often to follow an especially successful war chief. Quanah was probably attracted to the Kwahadies by their reputation as persistent and consummately skillful raiders. If so, he made the switch at a most opportune time, for the Comanches suddenly found themselves almost unopposed. The Civil War not only stripped the forts of U.S. soldiers, but also sent about 60,000 Texans into the Confederate Army, leaving scarcely 27,000 men behind to defend the entire state. The Comanches, together with the Kiowas and other allies, turned central Texas into a disaster area. Hundreds of settlers were massacred, and their settlements were reduced to charred ruins. When the U.S. Army finally returned after the war, an officer remarked, "This rich and beautiful section does not contain today as many white people as it did when I visited it 18 years ago."

The raiders' success was more apparent than real. The Comanche bands had not replaced the losses they had suffered in the cholera epidemic of 1849 or in the Texas Ranger attacks that followed it. So when the war-weary U.S. government called a grand peace council with the Indians of the southern plains at Medicine Lodge Creek, Kansas, in 1867, most chiefs were willing to listen — and eager for the gifts that went with the talk. However, the Kwahadies and part of the Kot-

sotekas — then the two strongest hostile Comanche bands, with about one third of the tribe's population — disdained the peace talks and sent no representatives.

Over a period of two weeks in October, the peace commissioners from Washington elaborated on their plans for the Comanches, Kiowas, Arapahos and Cheyennes: the tribes were to cede their homelands, go to a reservation in Indian Territory and accept government guarantees of land, rations and protection from hostile whites or Indians.

Ten Bears, a chief of the Yamparika Comanches, protested, "We wish only to wander in the prairie until we die." But more out of weariness than hope or conviction, he and nine other Comanche chiefs signed. The government conveniently interpreted these signatures as representing the consent of all Comanches. Henceforth the Kwahadies, whose fierce raiding warranted fierce retribution, would be attacked with special fervor for trumped-up reasons: for clinging to homelands they had not signed away, and for breaking a peace they had never agreed to.

During the council, Quanah, who may have been lurking nearby, sought news of how the talks were going. As an up-and-coming young warrior who looked forward to a future rich in battle honors, he was dead set against accommodation. In one debate with Comanche leaders, Quanah declared, "My band is not going to live on the reservation. Tell the white chiefs that the Kwahadies are warriors."

It was apparently during the Medicine Lodge talks that Quanah learned of his mother's fate. Cynthia Ann had tried repeatedly to leave the Parkers and return to the Comanches, but her well-meaning relatives kept thwarting her attempts. Then in 1864 her daughter Prairie Flower died of disease. Cynthia Ann, overcome with grief, starved herself to death.

From the first, the Medicine Lodge Treaty was honored mainly in the breach by both sides. The Kwahadies, having shunned the peace talks, ignored the treaty terms and continued their marauding. Quanah took part in one raid in the vicinity of Gainesville that nearly ended in disaster. The war party was intercepted by soldiers while en route home, and the Indians' leader was killed. Quanah distinguished himself by assuming command and using sound judgment in breaking off the fight. Thereafter he led several raiding parties as a war

At an 1847 peace council in central Texas, painted by the daughter of a German emigrant, Comanche chiefs grant a right of way through their

chief and participated in others as second in command to Bull Bear, the leading Kwahadi chief.

Meanwhile, the treaty-signing Comanches and Kiowas entered their shared reservation in Indian Territory. But they were soon embittered by their government rations of pork and cornmeal, by the Indian agent's efforts to teach them how to farm, and by the intrusion of whites and eastern Indians who stole their livestock. Before the decade was out, thousands of resentful Comanches were leading a dangerous double life: languishing on the reservation through the winter, then leaving in the spring to hunt buffalo and do some raiding on their own or with the holdout bands.

Washington did not tolerate this situation for long. In 1870, a crack Army officer was given command of the 4th Cavalry and assigned to put a halt to the raid-

ing in Texas; he was a 30-year colonel named Ranald Slidell Mackenzie, whose brilliant Civil War service had prompted General Ulysses S. Grant to call him "the most promising young officer in the Army." Grim, unapproachable and mercilessly tough, Mackenzie cared nothing for Army spit-and-polish. He allowed his troopers to wear dirty uniforms and long hair, and he told them to discard their sabers, which he regarded as useless. But he molded a force that could fight in the guerrilla style of the Indians under any conditions of terrain and weather. One of Mackenzie's early moves was to set up patrols out of Forts Richardson, Griffin and Concho, keeping men in the field at all times.

In September 1871, Mackenzie assembled some 600 troops for an invasion of the Kwahadies' home ground along the little-known Staked Plains. Soon after

land in exchange for $3,000 in presents. The pact hastened their downfall by persuading would-be settlers that Comanches were manageable.

hitting the trail, Mackenzie's command made contact with war parties led by Quanah and Bull Bear. The wily chiefs did not oblige Mackenzie by fighting a pitched battle. Arrogantly they pursued their pursuers across the plains, and from time to time small groups of warriors would make lightning thrusts at the long column and then wheel and vanish before the troopers could form ranks to follow them. Shortly after midnight on October 10, Quanah led a wild charge through Mackenzie's encampment, ringing cowbells and flapping buffalo skins to panic the cavalry horses. The stampede enriched Quanah with 66 prime mounts, including Mackenzie's own prized animal.

In the morning, Mackenzie sent a small detachment of troopers to try to recover the lost horses. They came upon the Comanches about three miles from the mouth

of Blanco Canyon. A group of warriors, with Quanah in the forefront, sallied forth to meet them. Quanah charged straight at the soldiers, killed one and dismounted to take his scalp while the rest of the overmatched troopers beat a hasty retreat.

The relentless Mackenzie continued to hound the Kwahadies into the Staked Plains. But on October 12, a howling blizzard put an end to the futile chase. Heading back toward home, Mackenzie spotted two Comanches observing his troops. He went after them and caught an arrow in the hip, a wound that incapacitated him for a time. It was a dismaying end to a frustrating mission, but he had learned valuable lessons about Comanche tactics and their highland refuge.

By March of 1872, Mackenzie was back in the field again, hunting Comanche raiders and keeping a

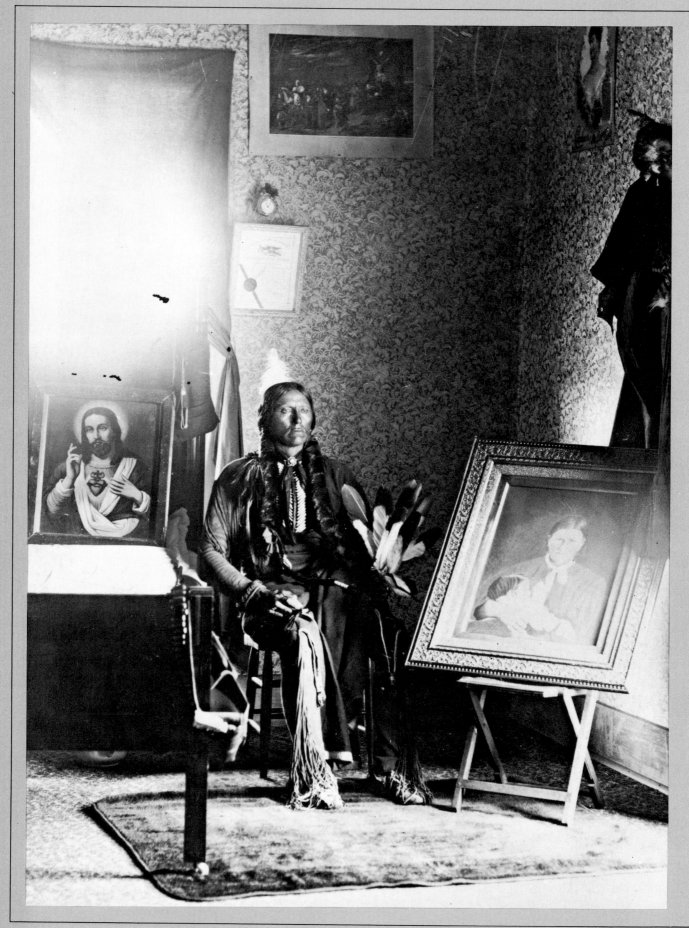

←⫷ Acknowledging his dual heritage, Quanah sits for a living-room portrait in his chief's finery, flanked by a painting of his mother and an icon of her people's "Jesus road" — a religion he respected but did not follow.

Five of Quanah's 25 children try, with mixed success, to smile for the camera in this 1892 photograph. All were encouraged to learn the white man's ways, and two of his daughters took white husbands.

Awaiting the arrival of guests at his breakfast table, Quanah assumes the place of honor beneath a large advertising poster, one of several used as decorations on his dining-room walls. Two of his wives are among those present, seated to his left.

At the ritual breakfast concluding an 1892 peyote meeting, food containers are formally aligned in front of the crescent-shaped peyote altar.

The peyote ceremony: a release from misery

Worldly wise in business and politics, Quanah Parker also exercised a leadership role in less mundane matters: he was a proponent of the ceremonial use of peyote, a hallucinogenic drug that offered solace to Comanches as reservation life eroded their tribal values. Largely because of his proselytizing, the rite began to spread widely among other Plains tribes shortly before the turn of the century. Ultimately it became the focus of an Indian religion known as the Native American Church.

The peyote rite centered around the eating of the bitter-tasting "buttons," or the aboveground part, of the peyote cactus, a spineless species about the size of a radish found in northern Mexico. The buttons produced auditory hallucinations, visions in refulgent colors and a deep sense of brotherhood among those participating. Peyote was also believed to possess curative powers, and it was this supposed attribute that apparently aroused Quanah's enthusiasm. Initially opposed to its use, he became a convert after attending ceremonies in 1884 and gaining relief from a stomach ailment.

A peyote meeting was held at night in a special tipi and ordinarily was ·

PEYOTE BUTTON

attended only by men. They seated themselves around a small clay altar, symbolizing the mountain range where, according to legend, peyote was discovered. After the leader of the ceremony distributed the buttons, sacred songs were chanted, accompanied by a drum and rattles. By the time the rite ended with breakfast at daybreak, each man might have consumed anywhere from four to 30 buttons.

Quanah frequently presided at such meetings, wielding ritual gear like the items shown opposite (the staff and the kettledrum may actually have been his). On one occasion, attempting to explain the peyote ceremony in terms a white listener could understand, he stated: "The white man goes into his church house and talks about Jesus; the Indian goes into his tipi and talks *to* Jesus."

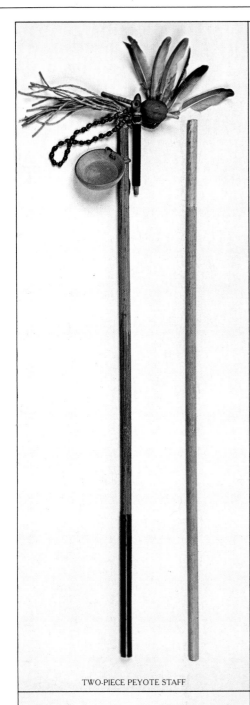

TWO-PIECE PEYOTE STAFF

FEATHER AND BEAD FAN

GOURD RATTLE

POUCH FOR PEYOTE BUTTONS

The sacred paraphernalia of the peyote cult, indispensable to the performance of its night-long rites, was provided by the leader of the group. As soon as the peyote was distributed from a distinctive buckskin-fringed pouch, the celebrants took turns singing to the throb of a kettledrum and the rattle of a pebble-filled gourd. The drum, the gourd and the long, symbol-laden staff —which might later be taken apart for convenient storage—were passed from hand to hand, along with a feathered fan that represented the birds linking God and man.

DRUM

4 | Protecting a way of life

While most tribes either bitterly resisted or reluctantly submitted to the white invasion of their ancestral wilderness, a few chose a third alternative — alliance with the whites. It was a course as logical to them as continuing to resist their ancient Indian foes.

Much like feudal Europe with its many tiny principalities, the West was a patchwork of tribes with no common language or culture. Each tribe regarded itself as autonomous, its customs superior, its members unique. Even the names they chose reflected their sense of singularity: the Cheyennes called themselves Dzi-tsi-istas, meaning "our people"; the Apaches were Tinde, or "the people"; the Kiowas were Ka-i-gwu, "principal people."

Because warfare among these proud nations was a way of life, the only hope of survival for the smaller tribes was to forge alliances with stronger forces. When the white men came, it was quickly apparent that they would make the most powerful allies of all.

No chief who chose this course was more steadfast than Washakie of the Eastern Shoshonis. A man of steely will, he would not brook any challenge to his policy of cooperation. When one of his sons was about to join a war party against the whites in revenge for broken promises, Washakie said, "My son, rather than see you take up arms against the white man, I will strike you dead at my feet." His son desisted.

The Shoshonis' friendship with the whites began with the visit of the explorers Lewis and Clark in 1805 and was fostered by more than three decades of commerce with beaver hunters who roamed their mountain homeland. Accompanying one party of trappers was Alfred Jacob Miller, a Baltimore-born artist who compiled a pictorial record of a tribe that found it possible to choose peace and yet stay proud.

In an idyllic panorama of the Shoshonis' high plateau country, a chief and two of his aides watch

from a bluff that overlooks the Sweetwater River while a party of warriors comes back from a marauding expedition against an enemy tribe.

Jubilant at the arrival of summer in her highland domain, a bare-breasted Shoshoni maid swings from a branch as a demure friend looks on.

Savoring a moment of solitude at the edge of camp, a warrior smokes his pipe — "the great solace of his leisure hours," said artist Miller.

133

Firing rifles as they gallop in a great processional circle around their camp, some 2,000 Eastern Shoshonis — according to artist Miller's estimate

— present a spectacular greeting to the fur-trapping contingent *(far right, middle ground)* that had brought the painter to the West in 1837.

ABRAHAM LINCOLN

JAMES GARFIELD

ANDREW JOHNSON

THOMAS JEFFERSON

Washakie–tough-minded ally of the white man

The event went almost unnoticed by newspapers whose editions were being otherwise filled with lurid stories about the rampages of the Sioux and Cheyennes on the northern plains. In the autumn of 1876 the U.S. government paid ceremonious homage to an Indian chief — Washakie of the Shoshonis. Unlike the Comanche war chief, Quanah, who had cooperated with the whites only after he saw that resistance was futile, Washakie had early decided that the best interests of his people lay in accommodation with the endless stream of foreigners who were invading his land and bringing a new civilization. And so from the outset he had given them his generous support — including invaluable military assistance.

It was as a reward for these services that Washakie was being honored by his allies in a remarkable celebration. The setting was Camp Brown, a military post on the tribe's 1,520,000-acre reservation in Wyoming Territory, and the natural backdrops were magnificent. This was mile-high land, just east of the Continental Divide, well watered by rivers and creeks, rich in game. To the northwest lay the Grand Tetons and Yellowstone National Park, established four years earlier. Not far to the south was the famed South Pass, where throngs of Oregon-bound pioneers, Mormons and forty-niners had breached the barrier of the Rockies. Washakie had done much to assure the safety of their passage.

Now, as bugles sounded, soldiers formed ranks on one side of the parade ground and Shoshoni warriors lined up on the other. Agent James Irwin stepped forward from a phalanx of Indian Bureau dignitaries and presented the venerable chief with a handsome saddle elaborately trimmed with silver. Then he started on a solemn speech.

This gift, Irwin said, was sent by the Great White Father in Washington, President Ulysses S. Grant, to his great friend in Wyoming, Chief Washakie of the Shoshonis. The President was aware that the chief had saved the lives of many emigrants by guiding them and providing protection against hostile Indians in the early days of the Oregon Trail. He was grateful, Irwin continued, that Washakie and his warriors had fought alongside United States soldiers against the Sioux and the Northern Cheyennes, enemies of the government, and he wished to express his particular gratitude for the aid given to General George Crook in recent operations against those enemies. Furthermore, he commended Washakie's efforts to educate the Shoshoni people. "President Grant," concluded the agent, "is one of your admirers."

Throughout the speech the chief remained with his arms folded and his face immobile. But tears welled from his eyes, and when it came time for him to speak he had no words.

Irwin prompted him: "What reply shall I send to the Great Father in Washington?"

Washakie still did not speak.

Irwin continued his urging: There must be something Washakie could say so that the President would know how pleased he was. A few words would do.

Washakie remained silent for a moment more, and finally he said: "When a favor is shown a white man, he feels it in his head and his tongue speaks. When a kindness is shown to an Indian, he feels it in his heart, and the heart has no tongue. I have spoken."

The agent expressed pleasure at this response. "That is just the reply I wish President Grant to receive,"

Chiefs who were friendly to the whites were rewarded with peace medals, minted by 21 administrations. Each issue bore the incumbent President's likeness on one side; the obverse usually conveyed a simple message of brotherhood. Lincoln's medal, however, offered a moral lesson: agriculture as a promising alternative to the quest for scalps.

he told Washakie. "Something out of the ordinary."

Whatever Grant himself thought of the old chief's words — and his reactions are not on record — every authority concerned with the Western Indians knew well that this chief and these people were indeed something extraordinary. While a number of tribes had voluntarily chosen not only to walk the white man's road but also to fight shoulder to shoulder with U.S. soldiers, none had done nearly so much to facilitate white settlement of the West as the Shoshonis. Their reasons were selfish, to be sure: the need for trade goods, the wish to be protected from powerful Indian enemies, and the desire to win favor with newcomers who seemed destined to inherit the future. Yet those motives were by no means craven or demeaning. One had only to look at Washakie to see that this was so. He carried himself with the dignity and quiet strength of a man who was a stranger to fear. Even the Sioux chiefs, Red Cloud and Crazy Horse — his enemies — acknowledged him as the greatest of all Indian warriors.

The friendship between the white man and the Shoshonis began at about the time of Washakie's birth, shortly after the turn of the 19th Century. The Shoshonis were then scattered from South Dakota through the Wind River country in present-day Wyoming, parts of Montana, Utah, Idaho, Nevada and California. Linguistically and culturally related to the Utes of the Colorado Rockies, and to the Paiutes of the Great Basin, they were a fierce fighting people who early acquired the horse and contested with the Sioux, Crows, Blackfeet, Cheyennes and Arapahos for mastery of the Montana and Wyoming grasslands.

The first meeting between the Shoshonis and the white man was an auspicious one. On April 7, 1805, the explorers Meriwether Lewis and William Clark, still in the early stages of their great 7,689-mile Western reconnaissance, set out from their winter camp near what is now Bismarck, North Dakota, and followed the Missouri westward into the virgin wilderness. With them was a guide-interpreter whom they had recruited during the winter, a French-Canadian trader named Toussaint Charbonneau. He brought along his young Shoshoni wife, Sacajawea, only about 16 years of age. She had been taken captive five years earlier by a war party of Hidatsas, and Charbonneau had subsequently

acquired her from her captors in a game of chance. Six weeks before the expedition got underway, Sacajawea gave birth to a boy, and for more than four months she carried the infant in a cradleboard on her back as she accompanied the explorers toward the Pacific.

When the party reached the headwaters of the Missouri, Sacajawea found herself in familiar territory, and on August 17 she caught sight of a group of her own people. As recorded in the journals of Lewis and Clark, she "began to dance and show every mark of the most extravagant joy, pointing to several Indians, sucking her fingers at the same time to indicate that they were of her own tribe." The expedition leaders proceeded cautiously into the camp, exchanged salutations with Chief Cameahwait, and sent for Sacajawea to serve as an interpreter. She came into the tent and had already begun to interpret when suddenly, the explorers related, "in the person of Cameahwait, she recognized her brother. She instantly jumped up, and ran and embraced him, throwing over him her blanket and weeping profusely."

This joyous reunion and Sacajawea's subsequent testimony to the good will of the white men completely won Cameahwait over. After the explorers distributed gifts of clothing, knives, tobacco, beads and mirrors, the chief gave them some desperately needed aid — pack horses to carry their gear and the services of Indian guides for their journey through the mountains ahead. The expedition left the encampment on August 19, having forged a friendship that would embrace virtually all whites who followed in their footsteps.

The boy who would be called Washakie was not then living among the Shoshonis. Only half-Shoshoni by birth, he spent his first four or five years with his father's people, the Flatheads, whose heartland was the Bitterroot Mountains of present-day Montana. After his father was killed in a raid by Blackfeet, his mother returned to her own tribe — a shift that seemed to afflict the boy with a lingering sense of rootlessness. In his early twenties, he transferred his allegiance to yet another tribe, the Bannocks of present-day Idaho, before finally settling permanently among the eastern branch of the Shoshonis a few years later.

At some point in his wanderings, his childhood name — Smells of Sugar — was replaced by the name Washakie, variously translated as the Rattler, Gambler's Gourd, Shoots Straight or Shoots on the Fly. In all like-

On a sight-seeing excursion in 1868, white families pause to visit a Shoshoni camp near the newly laid tracks of the Union Pacific. "It is good to have the railroad through this country," said Washakie, who had previously welcomed wagon trains, the Pony Express and the telegraph.

A quick stop by a junketing President

In the summer of 1883, a milestone was passed in Indian-white relations: for the first time, a United States President visited Western Indians on their own soil. The deserving recipients of this honor were the Shoshonis, whose friendship with the government had endured for nearly 80 years and who had been invaluable military allies. In actual fact, however, it was not gratitude nor even simple good will that prompted President Chester Arthur to travel to their reservation in Wyoming. It was trout. Suffering from poor health, Arthur felt he needed a quiet sportsman's holiday at Yellowstone National Park. In planning the trip, his aides scheduled a stopover at the Shoshoni agency —Fort Washakie—simply because its location and facilities qualified it as a suitable way station.

The President, accompanied by a dozen or so cronies, a 75-man cavalry escort and 175 pack animals, arrived at the agency on the evening of August 7. The following morning, Arthur dutifully reviewed a welcoming procession of tribesmen, witnessed a spectacular mock battle between the Indians and cavalrymen, then paid a call on Chief Washakie in his lodge. In a ceremonial exchange of gifts the chief gave Arthur a pinto pony intended for his daughter Nell; the President responded by grandly designating Washakie an Army scout — hardly a title worthy of a warrior who had led regiment-sized Shoshoni forces into battle against enemies of the United States. Despite this faux pas, Washakie presumably remained a gracious host; Arthur emerged from the lodge shaking his head and describing the chief as "amazing."

Forthwith, the President's party left for Yellowstone, where its members enjoyed a plentiful harvest of trout and bagged three antelope, a bear and a bevy of small game.

The next visit by a chief of state to a Western Indian tribe would take place two decades later, when another sportsman, Theodore Roosevelt, obtained relief from the pressures of his office by going wolf-hunting with a Comanche named Quanah Parker.

Shortly after his hurried but historic visit with the Indians, President Chester Arthur (*seated, center*) relaxes with members of his entourage in the locale that inspired the trip — game-rich Yellowstone Park. On his right sits General Philip H. Sheridan, commander of the Division of the Missouri, who had planned the President's itinerary.

Shoshonis — together with Arapahos who shared their reservation — line up to meet President Arthur. The chiefs hold umbrellas to distinguish them from ordinary warriors. Washakie did not attend; observing protocol, he awaited Arthur in his lodge.

145

exercise firm control over them to maintain his policy of cooperation with the whites. A not-always-benevolent despot, he literally dictated to his tribe and made free use of force to exact compliance. Frederick Lander described his brand of chieftainship thusly:

"He obtained his popularity in the nation by various feats as a warrior and, it is urged by some of the mountaineers, by his extreme severity. This has, in one or two instances, extended so far as taking life. 'Push-i-can,' another war chief of the Shoshonis, bears upon his forehead the scar of a blow of the tomahawk given by Washikee in one of these altercations."

Pushican, scarred as he was, fared better than a hapless warrior named Six Feathers, who was in the habit of beating his wife cruelly and often. An Army officer whose name and interest in the matter are not on record remonstrated with Washakie for permitting such uncivilized behavior. Washakie replied that sometimes wives must be beaten to make them obey. But such unmerciful beating, the officer persisted, showed that the chief did not have his people under sufficient control. Stung by this disparagement of his authority — and also ready to accept the white man's judgment that wife-beating was wrong — Washakie promptly went to Six Feathers and ordered him to stop. Two days afterward he caught Six Feathers doing it again, whereupon he shot and killed him on the spot. He, Washakie, was judge, jury and executioner, and few of his people disobeyed him more than once.

Nor did they successfully contest his leadership, although the size of his following fluctuated with the fortunes of the tribe and the inconstancy of the white man, who promised much in gratitude to the Shoshonis but did not always deliver. Many of Washakie's young warriors resented his close association with the whites and his increasing disinclination to take the offensive against Indian enemies. Some complained openly that he had become soft, that he was too feeble to win in combat and too much of an old woman to take enemy scalps. The war blood, they told each other, had ceased to flow in his veins; and they had begun arguing about who should succeed him.

Washakie overheard their rebellious talk. It angered him, but he said nothing. One evening he rode quietly out of camp to test his skill alone. A few days later, when he reappeared as unexpectedly as he had departed, he brought with him seven fresh scalps. He had been on the warpath, he announced, and had encountered a band of hostile Indians; these were the trophies he had singlehandedly obtained. "Let him who can do a greater feat than this claim the chieftainship," he challenged, holding up the scalps for everyone to see. "Let him who would take my place count as many scalps." There were no takers, and no more questions about his courage.

Despite his atavistic response to challenge, the percipient Washakie had been convinced for a long time that the Shoshoni life style of hunting and fighting was an anachronism in the new age that had dawned with the coming of the whites. Since 1858 he had been making known to government officials his wish for a reservation for his tribe. He wanted a settled homeland for his people, and nothing but the Wind River valley would do. Even though his native environment had been considerably affected by the hundreds of thousands of travelers who had passed through it on the overland highway, the Wind River heartland of the Eastern Shoshonis was by the end of the 1860s still rich in buffalo. It would offer an ample supply of food until the Shoshonis learned to grow their own crops and graze cattle in the fertile river valley.

In the summer of 1868, the government — in the person of Colonel Christopher C. Augur — finally granted Washakie his desire: the Wind River valley would be the Shoshonis' home forever. Before committing himself, Washakie went through each sentence and paragraph of the proposed treaty with the aid of two interpreters. He made sure that it provided for everything he considered necessary on a reservation: a school, instructors, a church, a mill, a hospital, farm implements and seed, and an Army post to help protect the Shoshonis against the powerful enemies who would, no doubt, come raiding.

On July 4, Washakie finally placed his X-mark on the treaty. "I am laughing because I am happy," he said, "because my heart is good. When the white man came into my country and cut the wood and made the roads, my heart was good and I was satisfied. You have heard what I want. The Wind River country is the one for me. We may not be able to till the ground for one, two or three years. The Sioux may trouble us. But when the Sioux are taken care of, we can do well." ◉

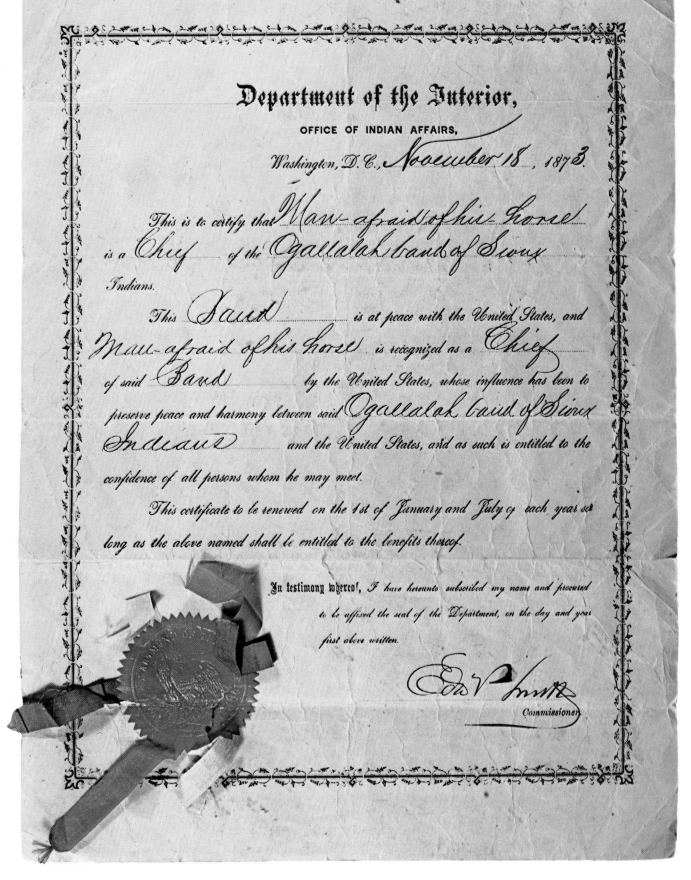

Department of the Interior,

OFFICE OF INDIAN AFFAIRS,

Washington, D.C., *November 18*, 1873.

This is to certify that *Man-afraid-of-his-Horse*

is a *Chief* of the *Ogallalah band of Sioux*

Indians.

This *Band* is at peace with the United States, and

Man-afraid of his horse is recognized as a *Chief*

of said *Band* by the United States, whose influence has been to

preserve peace and harmony between said *Ogallalah band of Sioux*

Indians and the United States, and as such is entitled to the

confidence of all persons whom he may meet.

This certificate to be renewed on the 1st of January and July of each year so

long as the above named shall be entitled to the benefits thereof.

In testimony whereof, I have hereunto subscribed my name and procured

to be affixed the seal of the Department, on the day and year

first above written.

Edw P Smith

Commissioner

147

Guadalupe of the Caddos not only called for his own people to accept white ways but also tried to convert other southern plains tribes.

Ute chief Ouray, an iron-willed autocrat, singlehandedly kept his militant band in line by shooting all opponents of his peaceful policies.

These last words were prophetic, for the Sioux and their allies would indeed have to be subdued before the Shoshonis could find peace in their Wind River valley. The Sioux were the most powerful Indians on the northern plains, about 20,000 strong, well equipped with firearms, and imbued with the spirit of conquest. For more than a century they had been moving steadily west from the headwaters of the Mississippi River. First they drove the Omahas and the Iowas from the coveted hunting lands in present-day South Dakota; then they swept inexorably on toward the Black Hills, where they confronted and overcame the Kiowas and the Cheyennes, compelling them to flee southward. In 1822, still on the move, they won a victory over the Crows and established their dominance over much of eastern Wyoming—within easy striking distance of the Shoshonis.

Washakie had a deeply personal reason for hating and fearing these neighbors. In 1865 a war party of 200 Sioux attacked his summer camp on the Sweetwater River, taking with them about 400 of the Shoshonis' horses. Washakie led a countercharge, driving back the enemy and recovering the horses, but in the engagement his oldest son was killed and scalped before his eyes.

Settling on the reservation brought the problems Washakie had predicted. In the spring of 1869, forty-five of Washakie's finest young warriors set off in search of a Sioux war party that had beset Shoshoni hunters in their Wind River hunting grounds. The Shoshonis caught up with the enemy but found themselves hopelessly outnumbered. In the bloody contest that followed, the Sioux swept the field and left all the Shoshonis for dead. Three of the 45, in fact, survived and reached the safety of their camp, one crawling 18 miles on his hands and knees in the snow to get there. A wave of similar incidents followed, and in September 1869, Washakie complained to the authorities at nearby Fort Bridger that "my reservation has been invaded many times by my enemy, the Sioux."

With these events to spur him on, Washakie drilled his warriors for long hours each day in mock battle tactics and cavalry maneuvers learned from his Army friends. He knew that his Shoshonis could not hope to handle the Sioux without the aid of a superior force; but some day, he was resolved, he would have his reck-

Resplendent in his war bonnet, Washakie looms over his tribal council in this studio photograph taken during the 1870s. During his six decades as chief, the council was merely a rubber stamp; Washakie told one emissary from Washington, "Whatever I do, the others will agree to."

Cradling a fan of eagle feathers, war chief
Medicine Crow poses for posterity during a
Washington parley in 1880 — four years af-
ter he and a force of Crows fought with
Washakie at the Battle of the Rosebud.

oning with the enemy, and he would be ready for it.

That day was still nearly seven years in the future. And when it came at last, it came because the white man had decreed it.

In the spring of 1876, Brigadier General George Crook of the Department of the Platte, regarded by no less an authority than William Tecumseh Sherman as "the greatest Indian-fighter the Army ever had," was selected to spearhead a campaign to subdue the bellicose Indians of the northern plains — the Sioux and their allies the Cheyennes. Crook had no intention of essaying such a mission with white soldiers alone. His extensive field experience had convinced him that a white army needed Indians to stalk Indians.

No white man had the Indian's intimate knowledge of his own terrain or his skill in tracking both animals and men. From the dust in the sky an Indian scout could tell whether what lay ahead was a herd of buffalo or a thousand warriors. From a faint trail of hoofprints, an occasional moccasin track, a patch of crushed grass and a scattering of pony droppings he could interpret the nature and size of the party, how long ago it had passed that way, where it had come from and where it was going. Broken branches, blazed trees and stones overturned without clear cause — all these might be read as Indian messages. A bird song or the cry of an animal could be identified as the forewarning of attack. And scouts organized into groups could also fight. Skilled in the quick skirmish, the darting attack, the capturing or stampeding of enemy horses, Indian scouts served as the military's guerrilla arm.

Thus, when General Crook received his orders to march north from Fort Fetterman in southeastern Wyoming as part of a three-pronged attack against the rebellious Sioux, he instantly thought to seek the services of the Shoshonis. And he was confident of a favorable response. Washakie had been waiting since 1865, when he had first offered the government his assistance in military action against the Sioux, for just such an opportunity to settle accounts with the most hated of his old antagonists. To Crook's emissaries he readily promised his wholehearted cooperation.

Meanwhile, Colonel John Gibbon had marched east from Fort Ellis in southern Montana. Early in April he met with the chiefs of the Crows at their agency on the Yellowstone River, with the object of recruiting scouts.

"I have come down here to make war on the Sioux," Colonel Gibbon told them in a cannily pitched enlistment speech. "The Sioux are your enemy and ours. For a long while they have been killing white men and killing Crows. I am going down to punish them. If the Crows want to make war upon the Sioux, now is their time. If they want to prevent them from sending war parties into their country to murder their men, now is the time. If they want to get revenge for Crows that have fallen, now is their time."

This prospect was so agreeable to the young Crow warriors that 30 of them went with Gibbon as scouts when he returned to his own camp, and another contingent promised to join General Crook two months later. As a result of their decision, the Crows found themselves fighting side by side with Washakie and his well-drilled warriors at the Battle of the Rosebud.

In the first week of June, Crook set up a camp and supply depot on Goose Creek, a tributary of the Tongue River, near the Wyoming-Montana border. Here he received a bold message from the Sioux war chief, Crazy Horse. Every soldier who crossed north of the Tongue River, declared Crazy Horse, would die.

Crook, now knowing approximately where to find the elusive Sioux, meant to cross as soon as his Indian scouts arrived. On June 14 he was joined by 176 Crows under their chiefs, Medicine Crow, Old Crow and Good Heart, and later in the day by 86 Shoshonis led by Washakie and two of his sons. Lieutenant John Bourke of Crook's staff was dazzled:

"A long line of glittering lances and brightly polished weapons of fire announced the anxiously expected advent of our other allies, the Shoshonis, who galloped rapidly up to headquarters and came left front into line in splendid style. No trained warriors of civilized armies ever executed the movement more prettily. Exclamations of wonder and praise greeted the barbaric array of these fierce warriors, warmly welcomed by their former enemies but at present strong friends, the Crows." Crook rode out to review them in their regalia of feathers, brass buttons and beads, "and when the order came for them to file off by the right, they moved with the precision of clockwork and the pride of veterans."

General Crook's total force now numbered 1,302 men: 201 infantry, 839 cavalry and 262 Indian fighter-

Outnumbered more than three to one, General Crook's forces try to fight their way through waves of Sioux at the Battle of the Rosebud. Though taken by surprise, the troopers managed a stalemate — but only because their Shoshoni and Crow allies bore the brunt of succeeding Sioux charges.

other eight days, to be exact, when they would meet and massacre a force of cavalrymen under Lieutenant Colonel George Custer, some 30 miles to the north, on the Little Bighorn River.

Washakie's contribution at the Battle of the Rosebud did not go unrecognized. It was shortly after his service to General Crook that he was presented with the gift saddle from President Ulysses S. Grant in the stirring ceremony at Camp Brown and was moved to unaccustomed tears.

He continued to lead Shoshoni scouts on the warpath for the United States until the defeat of the Cheyenne chief, Dull Knife, in the Big Horn Mountains late in November 1876. After that, he fought no more but remained on the Army payroll as a scout for as long as he lived. In 1878 he was again paid tribute; Camp Brown was renamed Fort Washakie — a compliment that pleased him perhaps more than any other.

As he passed his 80th birthday, then his 90th, his mind and his zest for knowledge continued to be as lively as ever. He spent part of nearly every day with the farmer-teacher assigned to the Shoshoni agency, peppering him with questions about the economics of farming and the correct utilization of water in irrigation. At regular intervals he rode off to the farthest reaches of the valley to inspect the farmlands of his people, and he frequently visited the school to inquire into the progress of the pupils.

Finally, blindness and the weight of his years confined the old chief to his log cabin beside the Little Wind River. On the night of February 20, 1900, Washakie called his family to his bedside. Straining to catch his fading voice, they heard him say: "You now have that for which we so long and bravely fought. Keep it forever in peace and honor. Go now and rest. I shall speak to you no more."

Two days later he was buried with full military honors at Fort Washakie. In the mile-and-a-half-long cortege that followed the flag-draped casket to the grave site were his own Indian police, employees of the agency, officers and soldiers of the fort, and all the grieving men and women of his tribe. When the coffin was lowered into the grave a squad from Troop E of the 1st U.S. Cavalry fired three volleys in farewell salute; and the poignant notes of "Taps" echoed through the hills that embraced Washakie's beloved Wind River home.

A delegation of Sioux moderates, visiting Washington for talks with President Rutherford B. Hayes in 1877, pauses in an art gallery during a gov-

ernment-conducted tour of the capital. Such tours were standard practice, planned to impress Indians with the white man's power and culture.

5 | Pacifist on the warpath

In the autumn of 1877, a missionary-reared Nez Percé chief called Joseph emerged as the tragic hero of a national morality play. The drama had begun 22 years earlier, when the tribe ceded a small portion of its ancestral range in the Pacific Northwest at the treaty council sketched here. This concession only whetted the whites' land-hunger. By the time Joseph became a chief, the government claimed about 90 per cent of the original tribal domain and was trying to evict his band and four others from the disputed land.

A pacifist, Joseph opposed both the white officials and the Nez Percé hotheads who called for war—until the Army attacked his people to put them on a reservation. At that, the chief took up arms. In a battle for freedom covering almost a quarter of the continent, his people won many a clash and earned universal admiration for their courage in the face of severe hardships. But they failed to win acceptance for the basic principle that Joseph voiced: "All men were made by the same Great Spirit. They are all brothers. The earth is the mother of all people, and all people should have equal rights upon it."

162

An unfinished watercolor by a government artist shows the colorful arrival of the Nez Percés at an 1855 peace talk near Walla Walla.

1840 and given the tribal name Thunder Rolling in the Mountain, was baptized by Spalding and given the name Joseph. He and his little brother Ollikut ("Frog"), born about two years later, spent much of their childhood around the Lapwai mission.

Under Spalding's stern tutelage, the Nez Percés became good farmers and cattle-raisers. But by the late 1840s, the increasing influx of white settlers, and the attendant rise in friction between peoples of different cultures, prompted Old Joseph to move his band southward to their ancestral domain in and around the Wallowa Valley. Joseph's Wallowa band and its four nearest neighbors were thenceforth known as the Lower Nez Percés because they inhabited the southern part of the tribal homeland.

In 1855, the U.S. government decided to settle the various tribes of the Northwest on reservations and thus clearly determine what land was available for development by whites. The Indians, including the Nez Percés, were summoned to a grand council in Walla Walla, Washington Territory. The Nez Percés' loose tribal organization, which gave a chief authority only over his own band, caused some problems in negotiations; government commissioners tried to simplify matters by designating one man as principal chief—an Upper Nez Percé leader whose persuasive oratory had won him the name Lawyer. In the end, however, this ploy proved unnecessary. Fifty-six Nez Percé chiefs, among them Old Joseph, signed the treaty, and it was a reasonably fair one. Although the tribe lost a small portion of its traditional range, the 10,000-square-mile reservation that remained was considered by the Indians to be room enough. In addition, they were promised $200,000 worth of goods in compensation for the territory they gave up.

These mutually satisfactory arrangements were disrupted in the autumn of 1860 by the start of a gold rush in Nez Percé country. Although prospecting was expressly forbidden under the treaty, neither the government nor the Indians tried very hard to stop the ragtag invaders. The Nez Percés gladly sold the prospectors horses and cattle, and patiently waited for them to go away. As the gold petered out, more and more miners did depart, some of them stealing Nez Percé horses in order to travel in style. But many whites remained behind as farmers and ranchers, and dissension

between them and the Indians increased dangerously.

Much of the trouble was over fences. Both whites and Indians would tear down each other's fences to use for firewood or to let their livestock through to other pasturage, whether or not the beasts trampled crops en route. But the Nez Percés' basic complaint was against the prejudice and inequities that characterized the administration of the Indian Bureau, the territorial officials and the white man's courts. Indians received stiff punishment for minor misdemeanors, while a white man could kill an Indian in plain view of other Indians but escape prosecution for the lack of white witnesses. The Nez Percés concluded that they could never receive justice from their white friends.

In an effort to ensure protection for the Nez Percés—and also to acquire more land for the whites in the process—federal authorities called another council in 1863. They presented the chiefs with a new treaty, which proposed to reduce their tribal holdings from 10,000 square miles to just a little more than 1,000. This prospect permanently split the tribe into two factions. The Upper Nez Percé chiefs, led by Lawyer, willingly signed the treaty. The agreement called for no sacrifice on their part, since their accustomed range lay within the reduced reservation, along Lapwai Creek. But the Lower Nez Percé chiefs, led by Old Joseph, were being asked to give up their homeland in the south and move north onto a reservation which, they maintained, was too small for the whole tribe. They refused to sign and departed in anger.

Back in his beloved Wallowa Valley, Old Joseph tore up his Bible—the "Book of Heaven" as he had always called it. This was no mere peevish gesture. The chief and other Christianized members of the Lower Nez Percé bands were so disillusioned by the white man and all he stood for that they quickly reverted to their ancestral nature worship, and they soon became susceptible to the preachments of one Smohalla, a medicine man whose so-called "Dreamer" cult had begun to spread through the Pacific Northwest. Smohalla's principal doctrine was that the Indians' lands were an inalienable gift from the Great Spirit, and it lent religious sanction to the Nez Percés' determination to keep their ancestral domains.

In the troubled years that followed, Old Joseph steadily failed in health, but his policy of passive resistance

was stubbornly maintained by his two very different sons. The younger, Ollikut—a huge man and enormously popular—advanced rapidly toward the status of war chief, winning many honors in his skirmishes with the Plains tribes, especially the Nez Percés' traditional enemy, the Blackfeet. Meanwhile Young Joseph —shorter than Ollikut, but nonetheless standing six feet two inches tall and weighing 200 pounds—took over more and more of his father's duties as civil chief.

Young Joseph's hardest chore was the futile routine of conferring with white officials and disputing their contention that the 1863 treaty obligated all Nez Percés, even the nonsigning bands, to move onto the reservation at Lapwai Creek. In the face of cajolery, orders and eventually threats, Young Joseph remained polite and friendly, but fearless and adamant. Though he earnestly desired peace with the white man and vigorously opposed Lower Nez Percé chiefs who spoke of war,

his intransigence convinced the authorities that he was the backbone of the resistance movement.

In 1871, Young Joseph inherited the full weight of chieftainship. As he later described his farewell to his dying father, the blind old man sent for him, took his hand and said, "My son, my body is returning to my mother earth, and my spirit is going very soon to see the Great Spirit. When I am gone, think of your country. You are the chief of these people. They look to you to guide them. Always remember that your father never sold his country. You must stop your ears whenever you are asked to sign a treaty selling your home."

Joseph buried his father in his beautiful Wallowa Valley, commenting: "I love that land more than all the rest of the world."

Who really owned that land? Major Henry Clay Wood, assistant adjutant of the Army's Department of the Columbia, made a thorough legal study of the ques-

Leaders of opposing Nez Percé factions were sketched at Walla Walla in 1855 by soldier-artist Gustavus Sohon. Lawyer *(left)* urged cooperation with the whites for "peace, plows and schools," while Old Joseph refused to cede ancestral lands.

tion and reported to the department commander, General O. O. Howard: "The nontreaty Nez Percé cannot in law be regarded as bound by the treaty of 1863; and in so far as it attempts to deprive them of a right to occupancy of any land its provisions are null and void."

But the legal rights of the nontreaty bands were of small concern to several key officials. Governor Lafayette Grover of Oregon wanted the Lower Nez Percés to vacate his state to make way for civilization. Indian agent John Monteith wanted them near him on the Lapwai reservation so that he could control them better. Early in 1877, the Commissioner of Indian Affairs asked General of the Army William Tecumseh Sherman to order U.S. troops to put the nontreaty bands on the reservation.

That May, General Howard called all of the Lower Nez Percé chiefs to Lapwai, instructed them to select land for their bands, and gave them exactly 30 days to

move their people, possessions and herds to their new homes. "If you are not here in that time," Howard warned Joseph, "I shall consider that you want to fight, and will send my soldiers to drive you on."

Chief Too-hool-hool-zote, another of the recalcitrant leaders, shouted at Howard, "I am *not* going on the reservation!" But Joseph persuaded the chiefs to avoid bloodshed as long as possible. Though the 30-day deadline was short, they rode south to comply with it as best they could.

Joseph's band, consisting of a few hundred people, hastily rounded up their nearest horse and cattle herds; the rest they would have to leave behind to be usurped by white settlers. Then they dismantled their village and bade farewell to the Wallowa Valley. On their way north, they had to ford the Snake and Salmon rivers, both of them swollen with melted snow. But they arrived just outside the Lapwai reservation with more than a week to spare, and there they camped with the four other nontreaty bands.

All of the chiefs and leading warriors met to discuss their predicament. Though members of the rebellious Dreamer cult taunted Joseph with charges of cowardice, he patiently insisted that war with the whites would be foolhardy. After the council, Joseph and Ollikut led a small party south to butcher some cattle they had abandoned in their rush to make the deadline.

While Joseph was gone, the encampment seethed with talk of war, which soon triggered violence in the band of the 70-year-old Chief White Bird. On June 13, a young hothead named Wallaitits set out with two companions to avenge the death of his father, who had been killed in a brawl with a white man three years back. The bloodthirsty trio failed to find the culprit, but they killed four whites—all of whom had committed some brutality against Indians in the past. Their triumph, such as it was, encouraged 21 young warriors to stage another foray. On this mission, they killed at least 14 whites, some of them were women and children. Throughout the region, farmers and ranchers fled in fright to the small towns.

The Nez Percés were frightened too. When Joseph returned to camp from his meat-packing trip, he discovered that many families, fearful of punishment if they now set foot on the reservation, were striking their tipis and preparing to flee. Though no member of Joseph's own band had been involved in the atrocities, he guessed correctly that individual guilt or innocence would not matter to the whites and that General Howard would want to thrash all five nontreaty bands. The peace-loving chief resigned himself to fighting if any Nez Percés were attacked.

During the next few days, Joseph urged all of the chiefs to adopt rules for humane conduct in case of war: stop the young men from killing women or children; let there be no scalping of the dead or slaying of wounded soldiers; if there was to be savagery in the conflict, let it be done by whites, not Nez Percés. The chiefs agreed to do their best to keep their headstrong young warriors under control.

Amid all the talk of death, one of Joseph's wives brought forth new life; a daughter, his second, was born just in time to detain Joseph as the bands scattered. One of the bands, led by the noted chief Red Echo, de-

cided to risk white wrath and go onto the reservation. Some of Joseph's people left with Chief Looking Glass (so called because he wore a small mirror around his neck) and camped with his band on Clear Creek. Chiefs White Bird and Too-hool-hool-zote, with their small bands, went to camp on White Bird Creek, and there Joseph joined them with the rest of his band as soon as his wife and infant daughter could travel.

Meanwhile, the white authorities began marshaling formidable forces to crush the rebels. General Howard sent messages by courier and telegraph to seven Army posts in his Columbia department, ordering all available soldiers to Lapwai. Outside his department, assorted troops were shipped from San Francisco, artillery units from Alaska, and an infantry regiment all the way from Atlanta, Georgia. Eventually some 2,000 U.S. soldiers, plus countless local volunteers, Indian auxiliaries and supply workers, would be brought to bear on the breakaway bands, which could not field even a tenth as many fighting men. On the eve of war, it seemed that the Nez Percés stood no chance.

That was the opinion of General Howard. He wired his superiors, "Think we shall make short work of it," and he quickly assigned missions to the troops already on hand at Lapwai. As a cavalry column departed on June 15 under the command of Captain David Perry, Howard saluted and called banteringly to Perry, "You must not get whipped."

Perry replied, "There is no danger of that, sir." Then the jaunty young officer rode off to what was one of the worst defeats the United States Army ever suffered at the hands of Western Indians.

Captain Perry's orders were simply to protect the refugee settlers who had flocked into Grangeville, a small town about 50 miles southeast of Lapwai headquarters. But Perry learned at Grangeville that Joseph, White Bird and Too-hool-hool-zote were encamped 15 miles away at White Bird Creek, and he could not resist such a golden opportunity. So Perry augmented his 103 cavalrymen with 11 civilian volunteers and confidently galloped off to punish the disobedient bands. At midnight on June 16, his men settled down behind a long ridge that overlooked the Indian camp. Perry was planning to take the Nez Percés by surprise at dawn, but the troopers soon learned that their presence

170

Members of the "Dreamer" cult that took hold among the Nez Percés by 1860 surround the prophet Smohalla (center, white shirt), who preached that the Indian dead would arise and drive the white man from their land. Joseph shared Smohalla's reverence for land, but not his antiwhite bias.

One-armed General O. O. Howard, who had promised a quick victory, doggedly pursued the Nez Percés from Idaho to Montana.
174

100

N
and
tern
ing
wate
shoo
impr
whe
back
on fo
dian
men
othe
mor

L
the
sieg
sitic
tren
the

C
that
eral
to a
gav
and
the
read
foo
new
bac
part
an a

tim
the
But
ject
mu
mia
us

are
dra
wa

Colonel John Gibbon, a veteran of campaigns against the Sioux, took a Nez Percé camp by surprise, and sustained a leg wound—and 40 percent casualties overall.

Colonel Samuel Sturgis, an Indian-hater since his son's death at the hands of Sioux, chased the Nez Percés through the Absaroka Mountains but failed to corner them.

Colonel Nelson Miles finally halted the Nez Percés just 40 miles short of refuge in Canada. Later, he championed Joseph's long struggle to return to his homeland.

party waiting for them on the far shore, just beyond rifle range. This insolent display had been planned by the chiefs to lure Howard's main force out of position and into a wild goose chase. The general obliged.

On July 1, Howard's troops crossed the swollen Salmon River unopposed and followed the bands into the dangerous mountains to the south. Although the Nez Percés were encumbered by their families and herds, they completed a circuitous 25-mile move in just 36 hours and, on July 2, recrossed the Salmon several miles upstream from their first crossing. Howard followed them to their second crossing point, but his ponderous column, unable to ford the stormy river there, had to retrace its whole agonizing route through the mountains. Not until July 7 did Howard recross the Salmon at the same spot where he had started his futile chase six days before. Meanwhile the Nez Percé bands had swung east, staging raids on Howard's thinly defended rear areas. In one attack, war chiefs Five Wounds and Rainbow wiped out an 11-man patrol.

On July 6, the Indians pitched camp on the South Fork of the Clearwater River. There they were joined by Chief Looking Glass's band and also by the band of Red Echo, who had been inspired to sacrifice the security of the reservation when he had heard of the victory at White Bird Creek. The five nontreaty bands were now all assembled together and at peak strength, with 150 men of fighting age, plus about 550 older men, women and children.

The Indians relaxed now, enjoying their successes, certain that General Howard was several days' journey behind them. They repaired their equipment, grazed their 2,000 to 3,000 horses and cattle, raided for supplies and skirmished on a small scale to keep the local defenders pinned down. The chiefs met to air their views on the situation, but since each band had the right to do as it pleased, the council made no special effort to agree on a course of action.

The days of respite were ended abruptly just after noon on July 11, when the Nez Percé encampment on the valley floor was startled by a cannon shot from the bluffs to the northeast. That shot, and the Gatling gun fire that followed it, announced the appearance of General Howard, who had finally extricated himself from the

184

A circle of tipis, at Nespelem in Washington's Colville reservation, was the last home of Joseph and 149 exiled Nez Percés. The chief, repeatedly denied permission to return to his native Idaho, said, "I have asked some of the great white chiefs where they get their authority to say to the Indian that he shall stay in one place. They cannot tell me."

6|The threatened world of Sitting Bull

When Sitting Bull was inaugurated as a Sioux chief in the 1860s, he composed a song for the event. "The chiefs of old are gone," he sang, addressing himself to the role he was inheriting. "Myself, I take courage."

An outstanding warrior, a revered spiritual leader, a wily politician, Sitting Bull parried every attempt to reduce the Sioux lands for as long as he could. When a white emissary urged him to go to a reservation and accept government rations, he answered bluntly, "We can feed ourselves."

Sitting Bull's great stature as a tribal leader stemmed in no small part from his gift for simple, almost poetic, eloquence. His words often reflected the inspiration that he drew from the ancestral Sioux world that he so passionately loved. Indeed, he once remarked that in the morning, when he walked barefoot upon its soil, he could "hear the very heart of the holy earth."

The Big Horn Mountains in Montana present a majestic backdrop for Sitting Bull's camp, which was painted in 1873 by Henry Cross.

From the Little Bighorn to Wounded Knee

Early in June, 1876, Sitting Bull of the Sioux made ready to supplicate the deity Wakan Tanka, the Great Mysterious. He scrubbed all paint from his face, bound the stem of his ceremonial pipe with sprigs of fresh-picked sage and, taking three witnesses with him, climbed a lonely butte and prayed toward the sun: "Wakan Tanka, save me and give me all my wild game animals. Bring them near me, so that my people may have plenty to eat."

These things he had asked many times, but now he wanted a more immediate favor. The Sioux were facing a showdown with the U.S. Army, and he wished for divine aid in battle — and perhaps even a portent of how the fighting would go. In hopes of winning his god's blessings, he made a vow to sponsor a sun dance, the most solemn of religious ceremonies. He further promised to offer up, during its performance, "a scarlet blanket" — a copious flow of his own blood.

All that could be done to ensure success in war had already been done. From this bluff along Rosebud Creek about 60 miles south of its confluence with the Yellowstone River, Sitting Bull overlooked an awesome assemblage of Sioux — perhaps 15,000 souls, among them some 4,000 fighting men. Most of the bands here belonged to the Teton Sioux tribal division that, for nearly a century, had dominated a range extending from the western portion of present-day North and South Dakota deep into Montana, Wyoming and Nebraska.

The great camp had no acknowledged supreme leader, but one man claimed the deference of every warrior present: Sitting Bull, chief of the Hunkpapa band, who could count more than 60 coups. True, there were

After the conquest of Custer, Sitting Bull was the most famed of chiefs — "the hero of his race," said an officer who knew him in the 1880s, when this portrait was made.

chiefs whose credentials as warriors were as great or greater. For instance, Crazy Horse of the Oglala band was considered a fighting man without peer. But Sitting Bull was something more, something extraordinary. He was said to be a familiar of the spirit world, which spoke to him in dreams or through animals. A member of his own band said, with stark simplicity, that Sitting Bull was "big medicine."

He needed all his gifts now, and all the guidance that his offering of blood might win, for the whites intended to crush the Sioux once and for all. Surveying almost three miles of tipis stretched out before him, Sitting Bull prayed: "Let good men on earth have more power, let them be of good heart, so that all Sioux people may get along well and be happy."

Sitting Bull was born in 1831 at Grand River, in what is now South Dakota, the only son of a Hunkpapa warrior called Returns-Again. At first, Returns-Again named his son "Slow" because, as an infant, he was deliberate in his ways, careful rather than abrupt in seizing food or objects. He kept the name only into the first years of adolescence.

Returns-Again was a mystic, as his son would be. On occasion he could communicate with animals. It was a gift of particular significance when it involved the revered buffalos, considered by the Sioux to be spiritual beings as well as the principal source of food, clothing and most things useful to man. One night, while on a hunt, Returns-Again and three warriors were squatting over a campfire when they heard strange sounds — a muttering vaguely like speech. As the noise came nearer they saw that it emanated from a lone buffalo bull which had approached their fire. After brief puzzlement, Returns-Again understood that the bull was repeating, in a snuffling sort of litany, four names: Sitting Bull, Jumping Bull, Bull Standing with Cow and Lone Bull. As

The spirited dance of the chiefs, registering the great esteem in which the Sioux hold their guest, is staged in front of the leader's tipi.

The vivid language of the Indian dance

In 1876, when Sitting Bull concluded that a final showdown with the United States Army was in the offing, he immediately sought spiritual guidance through the elaborate ritual of the sun dance. The Sioux resorted to a dance at virtually every critical moment for the tribe—and on many everyday occasions as well. Artist George Catlin, who visited the Sioux in 1832, was so impressed by their huge repertoire of dervish-like ceremonies that he said he was tempted to rename them "the dancing Indians."

Some of the dances that the artist captured on canvas during his sojourn among the Sioux were acts of supplication: thus, in the bear dance *(lower right),* hunters sought the forgiveness of a bear spirit, whose animal form they wished to slay. Other dances were strictly social; for instance, one understandably popular festival was staged to bring together young men and women under properly chaperoned circumstances. Another social event that gave Catlin particular pleasure was the dance of the chiefs *(above),* which saluted honored visitors—in this case, none other than the painter himself.

But the ceremony that most impressed Catlin was the scalp dance *(upper right),* a grisly pageant in which warriors celebrated victory over an enemy. The Indians, wrote the artist, "brandished their weapons, and barked and yelped in the most frightful manner, all jumping on both feet at a time, with a simultaneous stamp, and blow, and thrust of their weapons—as if they were actually cutting and carving each other to pieces."

A fortnight after Sitting Bull sought divine guidance in the sun dance, the Sioux staged just such a victory rite in the Big Horn Mountains, flaunting the scalps of cavalrymen who had been led by the vainglorious George Custer.

In a frenzied performance of the scalp dance, triumphant warriors wave freshly taken war trophies and re-enact their deeds of daring in battle.

Before a bear hunt, dancers, led by a medicine man covered with a bear skin, imitate the motions and sounds of their intended quarry.

Chiefs and white delegates meet at Fort Laramie in 1868 to hammer out a treaty pledging the Sioux a 41,000-square-mile reservation in Dakota Territory — plus clothing, rations and one cow per family. Cynical about such promises and uninterested in farming, Sitting Bull refused to attend.

205

my braids with both hands and tried to bite my nose off. He drew his pistol. I wrenched it out of his hand and struck him with it three or four times on the head, knocked him over, shot him in the head and fired at his heart." Custer's death was only one satisfaction of many. In the space of an hour, the Sioux had virtually destroyed the core of the 7th Cavalry. Custer's contingent of 215 men was completely wiped out. Indian losses were not recorded; but whatever the total, the victory was worth it.

It is not known whether Sitting Bull offered up any particular thanksgiving to Wakan Tanka for the day's outcome; he may have felt that he had already fulfilled his part of the bargain with his offering of the scarlet blanket. Nevertheless, he had reason for new concern before the day was out. He had told the Sioux that Custer's troopers were gifts from their god to be slain, but

he had warned against looting. The warning went unheeded. By nightfall the camp was laden with booty —cavalry saddles, uniforms, pistols, carbines and about 10,000 rounds of cartridges.

The battle had ended, and neither Sitting Bull nor his people would ever witness another day like it. It was a triumph, but it was also the beginning of the preordained end.

In September Sitting Bull witnessed proof that the looting of Custer's men would bring grief to the Sioux. The great assembly had split up in order to hunt buffalo more efficiently. General Crook's men attacked 37 lodges of Oglala, Brule and Miniconjou Sioux at Slim Buttes, only 30 miles from the Hunkpapa encampment on Grand River northeast of the Black Hills. By the time Sitting Bull arrived at the campsite with a relief force, it was too late. The village had been destroyed.

There were many corpses—young men, old men and women, children, babies—and the soldiers had also scalped some of the Indian dead. At Slim Buttes, the Army recovered much Custer property, including the 7th Cavalry's once-proud guidon.

In the aftermath of the defeat, some Indians gave up, but Sitting Bull did not and could not; surrender was not his way. About a month later, Lieutenant Colonel E. S. Otis, who was escorting supply wagons along the Yellowstone, received a written communication that was evidently sent by the Hunkpapa chief. "I want to know what you are doing on this road," it said. "You scare all the buffalo away. I want to hunt in this place. I want you to turn back from here. If you don't, I will fight you again."

Otis' superior officer, the veteran Indian-fighter Colonel Nelson Miles, decided to meet with the chief for a talk, hoping that he could persuade Sitting Bull to go peaceably to the reservation agency. The parley, arranged through an intermediary, began in a civil enough manner but soon degenerated into mutual angry suspicion. "No Indian that ever lived loved the white man," Sitting Bull declared, "and no white man that ever lived loved the Indian."

The meeting broke up and there was an exchange of shots. The soldiers, who had been the first to fire, drove the Sioux from the parley site and engaged them in a running battle that lasted for two days. The Indians counterattacked vigorously, setting fire to the grass and on one occasion forcing their pursuers into a traplike hollow. But Colonel Miles had artillery, which he employed with skill to keep Sitting Bull's forces from pressing too closely, and the 42-mile chase ended in a Sioux rout. In their flight the Indians abandoned camp

Sacred armor for a mystical cult

Within months of the founding of the ghost dance religion by a Paiute mystic named Wovoka in 1889, most Plains tribes had seized upon its promise of an imminent, all-Indian millennium and were regularly performing the dance — said to bring on a trance in which this glorious future might be glimpsed.

The movement had no more ardent followers than the Sioux; indeed, they probably introduced its sacred costume, the "ghost shirt," which was worn by both men and women.

The ghost shirts seen here come from various tribes, but their basic design is the same. Made of buckskin, muslin or cotton sewn with sinew, each garment is decorated with symbols revealed to its owner in visions. To the Sioux, however, the ghost shirt had a special — and ultimately disastrous — significance: they believed that it had the magical power to render the wearer invulnerable to the white man's bullets.

SIOUX

KIOWA

ARAPAHO

SIOUX

PAWNEE

SIOUX

SIOUX

ARAPAHO

SIOUX

SIOUX

drew his gun and fired a shot into Sitting Bull's brain. General gunfire broke out, taking the lives of six policemen and eight of Sitting Bull's followers, including his 17-year-old son Crowfoot.

And so it was nearly over. The wagon that came to carry away the bodies of the policemen also carried that of Sitting Bull. It was placed in a homemade coffin filled with quicklime and interred in a corner of the military cemetery at Fort Yates.

Nearly over, but not quite. The last tragic act of Sitting Bull's heritage and destiny still had to be played out and another of his prophecies had to be fulfilled.

The killing of the chief exacerbated the turmoil that was already sweeping the reservation lands. Bands of Sioux fled here and there, all badly frightened, many of them still holding onto the hope of deliverance through the ghost dance miracle. Some of Sitting Bull's followers, uncertain of the Army's intentions, hurried toward the camp of Big Foot, a Miniconjou Sioux chief who lived 100 miles to the south. They met up with Big Foot while he and his people were on their way to agency headquarters near Fort Bennett on the Missouri River to procure rations.

Meanwhile, the reservation authorities had decided that Chief Big Foot was a potential troublemaker and should be taken into custody. Colonel E. V. Sumner of the 8th Cavalry was ordered to make the arrest. When he intercepted the band, Big Foot gave assurances to the officer that their intentions were peaceful and lawful. Then why, Sumner demanded, had they taken in and sheltered hostiles from Sitting Bull's camp? Big Foot replied that he had found 38 men and women who were hungry, footsore and nearly naked in midwinter. Anybody with a heart would have done the same thing, he told the colonel.

Sumner nevertheless ordered Big Foot's followers, numbering more than 300, to accompany him westward to Camp Cheyenne, where they would be kept under his watchful eye. They obeyed his orders without protest until they had traveled back to the vicinity of their own village. The Indians then announced that

Bull Head wore this badge when he led the force that arrested Sitting Bull in 1890.

they would not go any farther. Big Foot advised the colonel that they intended to return home and that they had done nothing to justify their removal. But during the night, alarmed by some reports of additional troops that were coming from the east, Big Foot's people fled toward refuge in the Badlands.

Orders came from General Miles to pursue and apprehend the fugitives. Another cavalry unit caught up with them on December 28. Carrying a white flag, Big Foot approached Major S. M. Whitside to parley. Whitside demanded an immediate surrender, and Big Foot, whose band was in no condition to fight, gave in. The troops hurried the bedraggled band southwest to Wounded Knee Creek and took up surrounding positions as the Indians set up camp.

By morning, four more cavalry troops had arrived under command of Colonel James Forsyth, bringing the escort to 470. Big Foot was now ailing with pneumonia, and Colonel Forsyth provided a camp stove to keep the sick man warm.

In the morning, Forsyth prepared to disarm his captives. To secure the field, his troops were disposed on all four sides of the Indian camp, and four rapid-fire Hotchkiss guns were set into place on a low hill overlooking the camp from the north. About 8 o'clock the Indian men came out of their tipis and sat in a semicircle in front of the troops. Colonel Forsyth issued orders that they should return to the lodges, 20 at a time, and bring out their guns. The first contingent obediently entered the tipis but, after some time, reappeared with only two weapons.

Forsyth, concluding that the Indians would not surrender the guns willingly, decided to take them by force. Troops around the warriors were moved up within 10 yards; others were detailed to go into the tipis and make a search. The soldiers went at their work with hard-handed zeal, scattering bedclothing, pawing through other property. Women inside the lodges protested with shrill cries.

Outside, resentful uneasiness quickly edged into hair-trigger tension. Then a medicine man called Yellow

Red Tomahawk, flanked here by fellow Indian police, was one of the 43 men assigned to seize Sitting Bull. When his superior officer, Lieutenant Bull Head, was wounded, he took command and shot Sitting Bull in the back of the head.

DEC. 15, 1890. IND. POLICE K°. LITTLE EAGLE, AFRAID OF SOLDIERS, HAWK MAN, BROKEN ARM, W° BULL HEAD, SHAVE HEAD, ALEX, MIDDLE.
HOSTILES K°. SITTING BULL, CROW FOOT S.B. SON, BRAVE THUNDER & SON, CATCH THE BEAR, BLACK BEAR.
ASSINABOINE & SPOTTED HORN BULL.

CAPTURE & DEATH OF SITTING

In a fanciful 1891 lithograph, Sitting Bull, mounted on a white horse, meets a valiant end in pitched battle against soldiers. Actually, he was dragged from his bed by Indian police and shot when he resisted them.

Bird began blowing on an eagle-bone whistle and exhorting them to resist. When the soldiers began to search the warriors themselves, the situation exploded. A young Indian pulled a gun out from under his robe and fired wildly. Instantly, the soldiers retaliated with a point-blank volley which cut down nearly half the warriors. The rest of them drew concealed weapons and charged the soldiers.

Then the Hotchkiss guns on the hill opened up—on the women and children who had come pouring out of the tipis. Soon many of the tipis were burning, ripped by the explosive shells. A stumbling mass of women and children and a few warriors bolted into a ravine that led away from the encampment. The soldiers followed them, firing as they went. The Hotchkiss guns were then re-emplaced to sweep the ravine and cut down anything that moved.

Big Foot died as he tried to rise from his sickbed. Others managed to run as far as two miles from the camp before dying of their wounds. Twenty-five white men were killed and 39 wounded. Since the besieged Indians had few guns and since the troops were firing from four sides at once, it seemed likely that they caused many of their own casualties. The Indian dead numbered about 180. For three days they were left to lie where they fell while a winter blizzard swept over them.

A burial party was sent to the scene on New Year's Day, 1891. One by one the bodies, frozen in the grotesque agonies of death, were dragged from under the snow and heaved into a single pit. Four babies were discovered still alive, wrapped in their dead mothers' shawls. Most of the other children were dead. "It was a thing to melt the heart of a man, if it was of stone," said one member of the burial party, "to see those little children, with their bodies shot to pieces, thrown naked into the pit."

While collecting souvenirs, some of the men stripped the bodies. Beneath the outer layer of garments, several of the dead warriors wore the ghost shirts that were to have been impervious to bullets. Had he not already been two weeks in his grave, Sitting Bull would have seen here the final fulfillment of his vision during the sun dance on Rosebud Creek. To loot Custer's dead, he had prophesied, "would prove a curse to this nation." Custer's old regiment, the 7th Cavalry, had supplied the troops for the final holocaust at Wounded Knee.

225

228

Civilians hired to bury the Indians for two dollars a body pile the dead into a wagon, as cavalrymen keep watch for possible avengers.

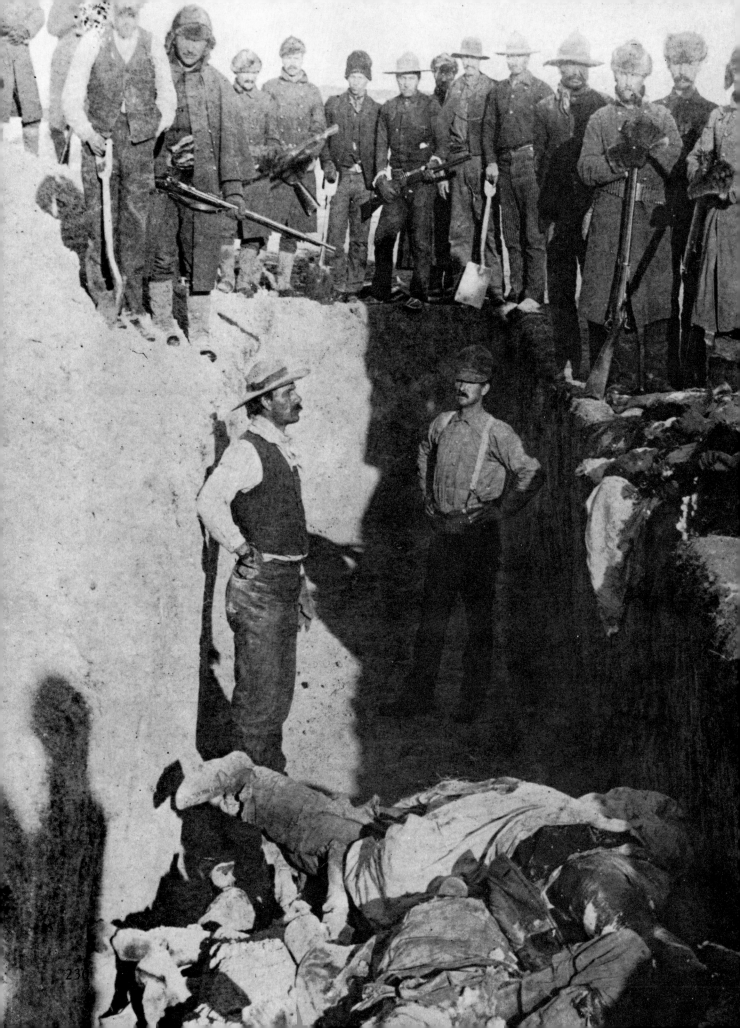

Burial workers pause while filling a mass grave dug on the hill from which cannon raked the Sioux camp.

Chief Big Foot lies slumped where he fell in the first moments of the battle, with a trooper's bullet in his head.

A

Adobe Walls, Texas, 114-116, *116-117*
Alchesay (Apache chief), *80*
Allen, Alvaren, 211-214
Alope (Geronimo's wife), 65
Apache Indians, 21, 26, 54-99, 130; Chiricahua band, 54, 57, 66-67, 68, 81, 86, 87, 91, 93 (*see also* Cochise; Geronimo); Jicarilla band, 26; Mimbres band, 63-64, 66, 68, 72, 73, *80*, 82-86, 91 (*see also* Mangas Coloradas); Nedni band, 63, 67; Pinal band, 69; White Mountain band, *80*
Apache Pass, Arizona, 73
Arapaho Indians, 30, 39, *42-43*, 109, 114, 139, 142-143, *144-145*, 196-197, 199, *218*, 219
Arizona Citizen (Tucson), 81
Arizona Territory, created, 78
Arizpe, Mexico, 67-68
Arthur, Chester, *144-145*
Assiniboin Indians, 182
Athapascan language, 64
Augur, Col. Christopher C., 146

B

Bannock, Indians, 139
Baptists, 41
Bascom, Lt. George N., 69-72
Big Foot (Sioux chief), 222-225, *226*, *232-233*
Big Tree (Kiowa chief), *35*, *36*, 36-41
Blackfoot Indians, 139, 142, 167; Piegan band, *13*
Black Hills gold rush, 199, 202
"Boomers" (1870s), 119
Bourke, Lt. John Gregory, 67; quoted, 154, 156
Bowen, Lt. William, 211
Bozeman Trail, 196
Bridger, Jim, 142
Brotherton, Maj. David, 211
Buffalo hunters, 112-116
Bull Bear (Comanche chief), 110, 111, 114
Bull Head, Lt. Henry (Sioux policeman), 220, *222*
Burnett, Burk, 119, 120
Butterfield Overland stage line, 68-69

C

Caddo Indians, 149, *150*
California gold rush, 23, 107
Cameahwait (Shoshoni chief), 139
Canada, Sitting Bull in, 180, 182, *207*, 211
Canby, Gen. Edward R. S., *186*, 188-190
Canon de los Embudos (Mexico), 87
Carleton, Gen. James H., 26, 73
Carlisle Indian School, Penn., *92*
Carrasco, Gen. José Maria, 65-66
Carson, Col. Kit, 26, 142
Carter, Capt. Robert, 103
Catlin, George, *6-13*, *22*, 101, *104-105*, *200-201*
Charbonneau, Toussaint, 139
Charger (Sioux chief), *12*
Chato (Apache warrior), *80*
Cherokee Indians, 23
Cheyenne Indians, 20-21, 30, 39, 41, *42-43*, 109, 114, 118, 130, 137, 139, 142-143, 152, 154, 159, 181, 196-197, 199
Chiefs, 6; qualifications for, 18-20, 21
Choctaw Indians, 23
Cholera epidemic (1849), 107, 109
Cincinnati Gazette, 30
Civil War, 26, 72-73, 109, 110
Clark, William, 130, 142, 165; quoted, 6, 139
Clearwater, Battle of the, 172-177
Clermont (Osage chief), *9*
Clum, John, 82-86
Cochise (Apache chief), 54, 57, 63, 66-67, 68-81, 87, 93
Cody, Buffalo Bill, 214, 220, *221*
Colville reservation, 183, *184-185*
Comanche Indians, 64, 103-105; and Kiowas, 15, 21, 23, 26, 30, 33, 34, 36, 39, *42-43;* Kotsotekas band, 109, 112; Kwahadi band, 103, 109, 112 (*see also* Quanah); Nocona band, 105; Penatekas band, 107; Yamparika band, 109
Congressional Medal of Honor, 80
Court of Indian Offenses, 124
Crazy Horse (Sioux chief), 139,
154, 156, 157-159, 195, 206, 211
Creek Indians, 23
Cremony, Maj. John, 65-66
Crook, Gen. George, 80, 83, 86-91, *87*, 93, 137; vs. Sioux, 154-157, *158-159*, 199, 206, 208
Cross, Henry, *192-193*
Crowfoot (Sitting Bull's son), 211, 222
Crow Indians, 139, 142-143, *149*, 152, 177, 180; vs. Sioux, 154-157, 196, 199
Culver, Charles, 72
Curly Headed Doctor (Modoc medicine man), 188
Custer, Lt. Col. George Armstrong, 159, 169, 199, 202; "last stand" (*see* Little Bighorn, Battle of the)

D

Dances (Sioux), *200-201. See also* "Ghost dance religion"; Puberty dance (Apache); Sun dance (Sioux)
Davis, Edmund, 37, 39
Dawes Act (1887), 212
Depression of 1873, 199
De Smet, Father Pierre Jean, 142, 197, *203*
Diseases, 21, 23; cholera, 107, 109
Dodge, Col. Henry, 23, 25
"Dreamer" cult (Nez Percé), 166, *170-171*
Dull Knife (Cheyenne chief), 159

E

Eagle's Ribs (Blackfoot chief), *13*
Eskaminzin (Apache chief), *80*

F

Five Wounds (Nez Percé chief), 175, 176, 180
Flathead Indians, 139, 177
Florida, Indians exiled to, 39, 41, *42-43, 44-53,* 80, 93
Forsyth, Col. James, 222
Fort Bowie, Ariz., *84-85*
Fort Marion, Fla., 39, 41, 45, *52-53. See also* Florida
Fort Richardson, Texas, 34, 37, 39, 110
Fort Sill, Indian Territory, 33, 36-41 passim, *46-47*, 93, 103, 119, 124

G

Gadsden Purchase (1853), 68
Garfield, James, *136*
Gatewood, Lt. Charles, 93
Geronimo (Apache chief), 6, 54, *60-61,* 63-68, 70, 73, 74, 80, 81-93, *82-83, 87, 94-99*
"Ghost dance religion," *214-215,* 216-220, *218-219,* 222, 225, 226
Gibbon, Col. John, 154, *175,* 178-180, *182,* 202, 206
Good Heart (Crow chief), 154, 156
Goodnight, Charles, 119
Grant, Ulysses S., 34, 38, 39, 81, 110, 137-138, 159, 199
Grover, Lafayette, 168
Guadalupe (Caddo chief), 149, *150*
Guadalupe Hidalgo, Treaty of, 68

H

Hanrahan, James, 114
Harper's Weekly, 165
Harris, Mrs. Caroline, *108*
Hayes, Rutherford B., *160-161*
Henry, Capt. Guy, 156-157
Hidatsa Indians, 139
Howard, Gen. Oliver O., 81, 86; vs. Nez Percés 168-169, 172-183, *174*
Huntsville, Texas, state prison at, 39, 41

I

Indianapolis, Ind., *50-51*
Indian Territory, 27, 29, *32-33,* 109, 110, 183. *See also* Fort Sill; Reservations
Indian Trade and Intercourse Acts, 27
Iowa Indians, 152
Irwin, James, 137-138
Isa-tai (Comanche medicine man), 114-116
Islandman (Kiowa chief), 15-18, 26, 41

J

Janos, Mexico, 65-66, 67, 82
Jefferson, Thomas, *136*
Jeffords, Thomas, 78-81, 93
"Jesus road" religion, 122, 126
Johnson, Andrew, *136, 138*
Joseph (Nez Percé chief), 6, 162-185, *164, 182*
Juh (Apache chief), 67

Jumping Bull (Sitting Bull's
adopted brother), 203

K

Kicking Bear (Sioux mystic),
216, *217*
Kicking Bird (Kiowa chief), 30,
34, 36-37, 39-41, *40*
Kientpoos (Captain Jack,
Modoc leader), *186-191*
Kiowa Indians, *14,* 15-41, *42-
43,* 130, 152, *218;* and
Comanches, 107, 109, 110,
114, 118-119, 124
Klamath Indians, 188

L

Lander, Frederick, 143; quoted,
146
Lapwai reservation, 166-168,
183
Laramie, Treaty of, 196-199,
204-205
Lawton, Oklahoma, 124
Lawyer (Nez Percé chief), 166,
168
Leavenworth, Col. Jesse, 26
Lewis, Meriwether, 130, 142;
quoted, 6, 139, 165
Linati, Claudio, *62*
Lincoln, Abraham, *136*
Little Bighorn, Battle of the, 200,
206-208, 209, 214, 225
Little Bob (Shoshoni warrior),
157
Little Mountain (Kiowa chief),
20, 21, *22,* 23-27, 30, 40
Livingstone, Dr. David, 30
Loco (Apache warrior), *80*
Lolo Trail, 177
Lone Wolf (Kiowa chief), 30,
31, 34, 39, 41
Looking Glass (Nez Percé chief),
169, 175, 177, 178, *179,*
180, 182

M

McCarthy, Sgt. Michael, quoted,
177
McClellan, Capt. Curwen, 34-36
McComas, H. C., 86
McGuire, Bird, 124
Mackenzie, Col. Ranald Slidell,
110-112, 116, 118
McKinn, Santiago, *88-89*
McLaughlin, James, 210, 220
Mandan Indians, *10,* 20
Mangas (Apache chief), *68*

Mangas Coloradas (Apache
chief), 63, 66, 68, 72, 73
Martinez, Jesusa, 69
Masterson, Bat, 114
"Medicine bundle" (Sioux), *198*
Medicine Crow (Crow chief),
154, *155,* 156
Medicine Lodge Treaty, 109,
114
Medina, Col. (Mexico), 66
Metal Breasts (Sioux police),
220-222, *223*
Methodists, 126
Mexican War, 68, 107
Mexico: Apache raids from, 86-
87; Apaches vs., 63-68, 81;
Comanche raids into, 86-87,
105
Miles, Gen. Nelson A., 91, 93;
and Nez Percés, *175,* 181-
183; and Sioux, 209-211,
220, 222
Miller, Alfred Jacob, *130-135*
Miller, Robert, 23
Mills, Capt. Anson, 157
Missouri Democrat, 30
Modoc War, *186-191*
Mole in the Forehead (Pawnee
chief), *11*
Monteith, John, 168
Mormons, 86, 137, 143
Mountain men, 142

N

Nachise (Cochise's son), 69
Nahlekadeya (Cochise's wife), 69
Naiche (Apache chief), *69, 70-71*
Nana (Apache warrior), *80*
Naretena (Cochise's brother), 69
National Indian Defense
Association, 210
Native American Church, 128,
129
Neecoweegee Indians, *7*
New York Times, The, 34
Nez Percé Indians, 6, 162-185
Noch-ay-del-klinne (Apache
mystic), 86
Northern Pacific Railroad, 199
North-West Mounted Police,
211

O

Oakley, Annie, 214
Oklahoma Territory, created,
119
Old Crow (Crow chief), 154,
156

Old Joseph (Nez Percé chief)
165-167, *168*
Ollikut (Joseph's brother), 166,
167, 169, 172, 176, *178,*
180, 182
Omaha Indians, 152
One Bull (Sitting Bull's nephew),
206
Oregon Trail, 137, 142-143,
146, 196
Osage Indians, *9,* 17-18, *20, 21,*
22, 23, 25, 41
Otis, Lt. Col. E. S., 209
Ouray (Ute chief), 149, *151*

P

Paiute Indians, 139, *214-215,*
216, 218
Parker, Cynthia Ann, 101, 105-
109, 119
Parker, Isaac, 107-109
Parker, Quanah. *See* Quanah
Parker, Silas, 119
Parker, White, 126
Pawnee Indians, *11,* 15, *148,*
149, *219*
Peace medals, *136*
Pecos (Quanah's brother), 105,
109
Perry, Capt. David, 169-172
Peta Nocona (Comanche chief),
105
Peyote ceremony, *128-129*
Phillips (Arizona rancher), 89
Pikes Peak gold rush, 23
Pile of Clouds (Nez Percé
medicine man), *178*
Plenty Coups (Crow chief), *149*
Plummer, Mrs. Clarissa, 108
Point, Father Nicolas, 167
Ponca Indians, *8*
Pony Express, 141, 143
Prairie Flower (Quanah's sister),
105, 109
Pratt, Lt. Richard Henry, 45;
quoted, 92
Puberty dance (Apache), *70-71*
Pushican (Shoshoni chief), 146

Q

Quakers, 38
Quanah (Comanche chief), 100-
118, *102,* 137; home of, *120-
121;* and reservation, 118-129
passim
Quanah, Acme & Pacific
Railroad, 126
Quapaw Indians, 183

R

Rainbow (Nez Percé chief), 175,
176, 180
Rawn, Capt. Charles, 177-178
Red Cloud (Sioux chief), 139,
196, 197, 199
Red Echo (Nez Percé chief),
169, 175, 180
Red Tomahawk, Sgt. (Sioux
policeman), 220-222, *223*
Reno, Maj. Marcus, 206-207
Reservations, 27, 70, 107, 109,
110, *147,* 212-213;
Comanches and, 118-129
passim; Nez Percés and, 162,
183 *(see also* Lapwai
reservation); Shoshonis and,
146-154; Sioux and, 192,
196-199, *208-209,* 209-
211, *214-225. See also*
Indian Territory; San Carlos
reservation
Returns-Again (Sitting Bull's
father), 195-196
Roberts, Capt. Thomas, 73
Roosevelt, Theodore, 93, 126,
183
Rosebud, Battle of the, 154-159,
158-159, 206
Ross, Capt. Sul, 107

S

Sacajawea (Shoshoni woman),
139
Safford, Anson P., 81
St. Louis World's Fair, 93
San Carlos reservation, *74-77,*
80, 81, 82-93
Santa Fe Trail, 23
Scribner's Monthly, 39
Shave Head, Sgt. (Sioux
policeman), 220
Sheridan, Gen. Philip H., 90-91,
114, *145*
Sherman, Gen. William
Tecumseh, 34, 37, 39, 73,
154, 168, 183, 188
Shoshoni Indians, 6, *130-135,
140-141, 144-145,* 199. *See
also* Washakie
Sieber, Al, 89
Sioux Indians, 19, 137, 139,
142-143, *147,* 149, *160-
161;* Brule band, 208;
Hunkpapa band, 195, 196,
206, 208 *(see also* Sitting
Bull); Miniconjou band, 208,
211, 222; and Nez Percés ,

180, 182; Oglala band, 195, 196, 208 (see also Crazy Horse; Red Cloud); Sans Arc band, 211; Teton band, 195; vs. U.S., 146-159, *158-159,* 169, 195-233 *passim;* Yankton band, *12*

Sitting Bear (Kiowa chief), 27, 30, 34, 36-37

Sitting Bull (Sioux chief), 16, 180, 182, 192-225 *passim*

Six Feathers (Shoshoni warrior), 146

Sky Chief (Pawnee chief), *148,* 149

Sky Walker (Kiowa warrior), 36-37, 39, 41

Smohalla (Nez Percé medicine man), 166, *170-171*

Society of the Ten Bravest (Kiowa), 27, *34, 37*

Sohon, Gustavus, *168*

South Pass (Rockies), 137

Spalding, Rev. Henry, 165-166

Staked Plains (Texas), 109, 110-112, 116

Stanley, Henry M., 30

Stieffel, Hermann, *18-19*

Strong Hearts (Sioux military society), 196

Sturgis, Col. Samuel, *175,* 181

Sumner, Col. E. V., 222

Sun dance (Sioux), 200, 202-203

Sutherland, Tom, quoted, 177

T

Taime (Kiowas), 15, 17, *21, 23*

Tatum, Lawrie, 37, *38*

Ten Bears (Comanche chief), 109

Terry, Gen. Alfred, 202, 206, 211

Texas, Comanches and, 103-105, 107, 109. *See also* Staked Plains

Texas Rangers, 107, 109

Theller, Lt. Edward, 172

Thorpe, Jim, 92

Tiffany, J. C., 86

Tombstone, Arizona, 86

Too-hool-hool-zote (Nez Percé chief), 168, 169, 176, 181

U

Union Pacific Railroad, 141

U.S. Army: vs. Apaches, 68-81; vs. Comanches, 100-129 *passim;* vs. Modocs, *186-191;* vs. Nez Percés, 165-185; vs. Sioux, 146-157, *158-159,* 169, 195-233 *passim*

U.S. Congress, 103, 183, 211, 216; Congressional Medal of Honor, 80; Dawes Act, 212. *See also* Reservations

U.S. Department of the Interior, *147;* Bureau of Indian Affairs (*see* Reservations)

Ute Indians, 15, 17, 26, 139, 149, *151*

V

Victoria, Queen (England), 211, 214

Victorio (Apache warrior), *80*

Vilas, William, 216

W

Wakan Tanka (Sioux deity), 195, 203, 208

Waggoner, Dan, 119

Wallaitits (Nez Percé youth), 169

Walla Walla Treaties, *162-163,* 166, 167

Wallace, James, 69, 72

Walsh (hostler), 72

Ward, John, 69, 72

Warm Springs agency (Apaches), 82-86

Washakie (Shoshoni chief), 6, 130, 137-159, *138, 152-153*

Wasp (journal), *173*

Weapons: Apache, *64-65, 88-89;* Comanche, *106*

Weldon, Mrs. Catherine, *210*

West, Brev. Gen. Joseph, *73*

White Bear (Kiowa chief), 26, 27-34, *35-36,* 36-41

White Bird (Nez Percé chief), 169, 177, 178-180, 182-183

White Bull (Sitting Bull's nephew), 207-208

Whitside, Maj. S. M., 222

Wichita Indians, 23

Wind River valley (Shoshonis), 146-154, 159

Wolf Chief (Mandan chief), *10*

Wood, Maj. Henry Clay, 167-168

Wounded Knee, Battle of, 222-225, *226-233*

Wovoka (Paiute mystic), 216, 218

Y

Yellow Bird (Sioux medicine man), 222-225

Yellowstone National Park, 137, *144-145,* 180

Young, Brigham, 143

Yuman Indians, 64

Z

Zotom (Kiowa youth), *44-53*

Zuñi Indians, 64